Temptation:
LESSONS FROM TRIALS IN THE WILDERNESS

A REVELATION OF THE WILDERNESS TRIALS OF JESUS IN MATTHEW 4:1-11

IRA POPE

DISCIPLESHIP SERIES: VOLUME 1

WESTBOW°
PRESS
A DIVISION OF THOMAS NELSON
& ZONDERVAN

Scripture references taken from the King James Version
of the Bible unless otherwise noted.

Scriptures taken from the Holy Bible, New International Version®, NIV®.
Copyright © 1973, 1978, 1984, 2011 by Biblica, Inc.™ Used by permission
of Zondervan. All rights reserved worldwide. www.zondervan.com The
"NIV" and "New International Version" are trademarks registered in
the United States Patent and Trademark Office by Biblica, Inc.™

Author Credits: Thank you to the Holy Spirit of Truth for revealing
rhema truths for the deliverance of many, and special thanks to my
wonderful prayer partners around the world whose diligent faithful prayers
have indeed been instrumental in the completion of this work.

WestBow Press books may be ordered through booksellers or by contacting:

WestBow Press
A Division of Thomas Nelson & Zondervan
1663 Liberty Drive
Bloomington, IN 47403
www.westbowpress.com
1 (866) 928-1240

ISBN: 978-1-4908-2206-8 (sc)
ISBN: 978-1-4908-2207-5 (hc)
ISBN: 978-1-4908-2266-2 (e)
Library of Congress Control Number: 2014900339

Printed in the United States of America.
WestBow Press rev. date: 02/11/2014

This book is dedicated to my beloved Grandparents Donald and Alma Turner, and Uncles Eric Turner and Maurey Richards. I pray every day for your knowledge of God's Truth and faith in Him to continue to grow.

A Kingdom Meal for Spiritual Nourishment

"My meat is to do the will of him that sent me,
and to finish his work." John 4:34 KJV

Take my yoke upon you and learn of Me, for I
am gentle and humble in heart, and you will find
rest for your souls. Matthew 11:29 NIV

"For the kingdom of God is not meat and
drink; but righteousness, and peace, and joy
in the Holy Ghost." Romans 14:17 KJV

Revelation Menu
(Table of Contents)

Kingdom Meal for Spiritual Nourishment

1. Living Water ix

2. Bread and Oil xiii

3. First Course: The Wilderness 1

4. Second Course: Fasting and Prayer 11

5. Third Course: Perspective 26

6. Fourth Course: Know Your Enemy 41

7. Fifth Course: The Lies of Babylon 63

8. Final Course: Cadence 100

LIVING WATER

Suddenly you are awake. Fighting for clarity through the cobwebs, you try to recall what and how exactly you were awakened. It seemed like it was the sound of a strong wind that grew louder and louder until the moment you opened your eyes, and then silence. Yet even though it's not audible, the intrusion still carries an escalating if uncertain immediacy. You turn your head just in time to catch, through still-focusing vision, the source of the only light in the room morph from 3:00 a.m. to 3:01 a.m.

A slow, deep, diaphragm-stretching inhale and pause … a moment of truth.

How tempting it is to roll over and grab (or steal, as the case may be if you are married) the other pillow and try to stuff it in the only ear that's free. See if that takes care of that sense of urgency now growing even louder inside your heart in the midst of the twilight silence of your bedroom. Or you could exhale with purpose, rising up and marching into your prayer closet, eager to answer the call of the Spirit to intercede for someone you may not even know.

***

The phone rings. It's a good friend named Jerry, whom you haven't seen in three months. He wants to get together and invites you to a mutual friend Ryan's celebration for receiving a coveted promotion. The plan is to meet up at a few of Ryan's favorite bar hangouts to congratulate him. The thing is, the reason you haven't spoken to Jerry in the last few months is because the last time you spoke with him, you expressed a deep concern for the increasing amount and frequency with which Jerry has been indulging in alcohol consumption. You also expressed how, as his friend, you refuse to witness it taking an increasingly negative toll on his life hoping that the move would help awaken Jerry to the seriousness of his problem.

The temptation is to take Jerry up on the invite, both to see him again and to congratulate Ryan. After all, it is Ryan's special occasion, as Jerry says. But the reality is you know that the "occasion" of summer, or the "occasion" of the imminent end of summer is a special enough "occasion" for Jerry to get full-on drunk. You really don't want to lose complete touch with your friend, but something has to give. Will it be you?

***

On your drive home from a particularly animated and stress-laden workday, you notice a potentially irritating traffic jam forming up ahead in your direction of travel, so you decide to exit and seek a detour. Longing to unwind and release the stress you feel lingering in your shoulders, you are relieved to discover this unrehearsed detour actually seems to be saving you time, with fewer stops than you normally have. Just as you begin to reenter familiar territory, you happen upon an old-time favorite Dairy Queen ice cream and treats restaurant you had not noticed before. After a trying day like today, it is particularly enticing, not to mention there is a drive-thru!

Just then it dawns on you that you have nearly reached the end of your second week of a new healthy eating program and have not strayed from it even once the entire thirteen days. The temptation is to heed what your mind is trying to rationalize—that you have been so good for almost two whole weeks, so you've earned the right to enjoy yourself. Besides, after such a tough and pressure-filled day, you deserve that hot fudge caramel sundae. It would be the perfect reward and would even help you to unwind and feel better. You could at least go inside just to see if anybody you know is working there, and go from there....

***

BREAD AND OIL

The Lord Jesus Christ is called by many names in the Bible: the Messiah, the Lamb of God, Wonderful Counselor, the Mighty God, the Everlasting Father, the Prince of Peace (Isaiah 9:6), the Savior ... the list goes on. The Devil is also called by many descriptive names. At one point his name was Lucifer, meaning "bearer of light" or "son of the morning" (Isaiah 14:12). That was his first, God-given name. Then, once he blew it and got banished from heaven for high treason, he was given the name Satan, which translates as the Opposer, or one who stands against.

Satan is also called in various places in the Bible the Serpent, the Dragon, the Evil One, the Enemy, and the Father of Lies, to name just a few. (It would seem the Devil also gets a few more unmentionable names from people who holler out after an accidentally kicked bedpost or coffee table at night as well, but thankfully those are rarely recorded.) Another of the more descriptive names attributed to the Devil is Tempter (Matt. 4:3). This name accurately describes the method the Devil uses to attempt to ensnare his victims—people—and trap them inside the prison of their own minds.

As the Tempter, Satan uses whatever vice he observes his chosen victim is most susceptible to. With that vice, Satan begins his typical assault by repetitively and continuously sending seductive messages to lure his victims through their minds. Indeed, his desired end result often manifests itself as sin conducted with or performed in the body, but the Devil's war is waged against the soul of man, in the mind. That is where the Enemy tries to build up strongholds, or mental funnels of warped and perverted reasoning. This is to keep people's minds boxed into carnal patterns of sin-based perceptions and thought processes.

Many of the Devil's worst, most ferocious attacks are not the ones that come with direct force, trying to make you give in to a certain act right at that instant. Satan certainly does that too, every time you see the advertisement of a pack of cigarettes, for instance, or pass by a liquor store, if that is your particular vice. But the deadliest, most effective attacks are in the strongholds the Devil goes about patiently building up in your mind subtly over a long period of time and often with the aid of this worldly society he has constructed.

For example, the Bible says God has not given us a spirit of fear but of power, love, and a sound mind (2 Tim. 1:7). However, if we listen to enough of those pharmaceutical commercials, and sometimes if we heed the misguided advice of the people in our lives, after years, and even decades, their repetitive and often-degrading words can eventually have us doubting the soundness of our minds and seeking all manner of sedatives and other prescription or non-prescription drugs. It is this sort of subtle, patient, and relentless attack of the Devil that can often have the most damaging effect on people's psyches, on their perception of the world, and on their perception of themselves.

If Satan can gain influence and control the believer's self-perception, he can harness us like a broken mule. Since he can't simply kill us, or we'd all be dead already, the next best thing for him is subduing our lives into self-interested flatlines of complacency. Or on the other hand, the Devil can manipulate us through lies, as he is also called the Deceiver of the whole world (Revelation 12:9), getting even some self-described Christian believers to do his evil bidding for as long as they allow him to. They are then the Devil's puppets, whether they realize it or not, until they awaken to the true reality of who they are—extremely powerful children of the most high God and heir to His throne, joint heirs in Christ Jesus (Romans 8:17).

The self-perception—in particular a Christian's self-perception—is what Satan attacks most ferociously. If he can win that battle, causing doubt or confusion in who the believers really are and what God made them to become at rebirth, he can prevent them from engaging their divine purpose. The Devil then has at the very least effectively rendered the believer obsolete in terms of his operation and has turned them and their Christian's walk into stagnant, stale couch potatoes. Physical death at that point is merely academic because once the Spirit fizzles and its fire is quenched, the mind and the body follow soon enough. For however long the mind and body remain, they are no more meaningful than a plank of wood being tossed to and fro in the waves of life.

Instead, believers must become fully enlightened to the revelation of who God created us to be, formed us in our mothers' wombs to be, and reformed us in Christ Jesus to be (predestining us in Jesus even before the foundations of the world, as Ephesians 1:4 says). Once Christians realize that we are, in fact, sons and daughters of God, kings and queens who should be reigning over all the earth, and coheirs with Jesus Christ to the throne of grace, then there is literally and conceptually nothing that will be impossible for us. No evil trick, no deceptive snare, no wicked scheme, and no temptation of the Devil can affect the righteous Christian (not self-righteous, but Christ-made and grace-made-righteous) who becomes fully aware of the kingdom of God majesty and power working in and through him or her at all times. We instantly become Satan's worst nightmare!

As Christians study the bible to grow in faith, we learn more about Jesus, and the Holy Spirit illuminates for us who God our Father really is, which in turn reveals the truth of who we are in relation to the Heavenly Father. The believer's divine sonship self-perception is the launching pad to his divine destiny.

Kingdom Nourishment for Spiritual Growth

FIRST COURSE
THE WILDERNESS

"Then Jesus was led up of the Spirit into the wilderness to be tempted of the devil" (Matt. 4:1 KJV).

This first time Jesus was led by the Spirit of God post-baptism into the wilderness, a picture developed of Jesus hearing God the Father's instructions through the Holy Spirit and then following them. The Spirit leads with instructions directly from the mouth of the Father, Jehovah, Yahweh, Elohim, El Shaddai—and Jesus obeys. This is clearly a display of the chain of obedience for us believers, the body of Christ, to follow. God's instructions to the Holy Spirit were to lead Jesus into the wilderness for the explicit purpose of Him being tempted. Since there are no accidents with God because He is perfectly purposeful (Isaiah 55:11; Romans 8:28 KJV), we can know that there was a specific reason God desired the wilderness to be the location for Jesus' temptation.

Two questions surface: why the temptation, and why the wilderness?

The Holy Spirit through the apostle Paul said in his letter to the Hebrews, "For we have not an high priest which cannot be touched with the feeling of our infirmities; but was in all points tempted like as we are, yet without sin. Let us therefore come boldly before the throne of grace that we might obtain mercy and find grace to help in time of need" (Hebrews 4:15–16 KJV). God the Father, in His perfect, extratemporal wisdom, saw fit to have Jesus tested and tried just like every human is tested and tempted so we believers can know the compassion Jesus has and God has for us is as real as the very trials we are going through.

Therefore, as we look to Him for our strength, we can take comfort in the fact that Jesus has already overcome the world (John 16:33 KJV). So then are we also overcomers through Him, prevailing through our circumstances by the strength of His Spirit. It is by God's grace, which He has made available to us, that we are already overcomers even in the very trial before us, so we don't have to wait until the end to rejoice. Since we are already victorious, we can celebrate in advance and give thanks even in the midst of the rage. Thereby, we receive the grace to make it through victoriously to the other side (Romans 8:35-37; Hebrews 4:14-16 KJV).

As our High Priest, Jesus has experienced every emotion, every suffering, every endurance, and every feeling we have, and then some, up to and including the ultimate betrayal by a beloved brother whom the Lord had hand selected to be a part of His very special group of twelve disciples. Jesus had even shared a flesh-and-blood covenant with this Judas to be part of Jesus' divine ordinance as the Messiah who would provide salvation for the entire world. Judas did not only deny Jesus like Peter did even with swearing. Judas actually *sold* Jesus out for 30 pieces of silver. The Savior was indeed touched with the feelings of all of our infirmities, and throughout His earthly ministry, He humbly and patiently showed us and taught us how we too can overcome our own trials without sinning (Matthew 11:29 KJV).

The book of Hebrews also reveals that Jesus took the divinely orchestrated opportunity embedded in trials and sufferings to learn lessons of patience and obedience, which worked together to make Him perfect (Hebrews 5:8–9; James 1:3 KJV). This process of Jesus being made perfect is our very same process of sanctification unto obedience, which through faith makes us perfect as well, in Christ Jesus (Hebrews 3:6-8, 14, 5:9, 6:1 KJV). In other words, in Jesus, we are made holy, so be holy. In Jesus, we are made righteous, so be righteous. In Jesus, we are made perfect, so be perfect. In Jesus we are made victorious, so walk in victory (Leviticus 11:44, 19:2; Matthew 3:8–11, 15, 4:17, 5:17–20, 48; Ephesians 1:4, 2 Timothy1:9-10 KJV).

God's instruction to the Holy Spirit was to lead Jesus, the Anointed One, into the wilderness to be tempted. Since God is perfectly purposeful in all He does (Ephesians 1:8–12 KJV), we can faithfully know there was a specific reason God wanted Jesus in the wilderness for and during this temptation season. What was the reason for the temptation taking place in the wilderness?

The separation, the solitude and the Sonship shield that existed in the midst of the wilderness would play key roles in the tempting of the Savior.

The wilderness of Matthew 4:1–11 was representative of Satan's domain (Isaiah 14:15–17, 27:10–11 KJV). We will investigate this in detail in a moment. That God chose this wilderness as the proving grounds for the building up of Jesus' faith and the working of His patience unto perfection (James 1:4; 2 Peter 1:3–8 KJV) reveals that He desired mankind, who are trudging through the wilderness of the post-Eden (Adamic blunder) Earth, to follow the example set by Jesus. As our Messiah successfully navigates through His appointed wilderness trial and overcomes the wilderness without sinning, we learn from Him to navigate victoriously in ours as well.

The wilderness event also serves as a clear foreshadowing of the final earthly trial the Lord would endure at Golgotha. Truly this trial and the overcoming of it were to be a living portrait of Jesus' mission, His purpose. As the obedient human Son, which Jesus had become, He would remain loyal to His Father's divine directive to rectify Adam's breach, to overcome the world and to redeem mankind from Satan's own doomed destiny, as well as to save mankind from itself.

Separation into the Wilderness

While God the Father designed many, if not most of the miraculous, kingdom of God occurrences in the earthly ministry of Jesus to immediately encourage and develop the disciples' faith, Jesus' temptation in the wilderness was clearly not another such drill. God the Holy Spirit had just descended like a dove on the freshly baptized body of the Messiah Jesus while God the Father's voice boomed from heaven, declaring Jesus' divine Sonship and God the Father's pleasure in Him (Matthew 3:16–17 KJV). The occurrence of this magnificent manifestation of the divine trinity, in the obvious presence of Jesus' disciples and followers and all bystanders, was clearly a soul-winning, faith-building miracle (Isaiah 42:1; John 1:51; Acts 1:22; Romans 10:17; Ephesians 2:8–9 KJV). Following this audible and visually tangible manifestation of the Trinity, the buzz throughout the land, and particularly in Jesus' camp, would surely have resembled a veritable beehive concerning what everyone had just witnessed. Faith was built (at least for the moment).

As we found out, God the Father now desired to begin facilitating the complete and effective temptation of Jesus. For that to occur, during these wilderness trials Jesus could not be readily conscious of those miracles or the reasons behind them because they point directly to His Sonship. As mentioned, with full revelation of the power of divinely appointed sonship, temptations have no effect. Therefore, the separation into the wilderness, away from those who would certainly be questioning and reminding Jesus at every occasion of the confirming manifestation, which they all bore witness to, was a necessity at this point in pursuing the will of God the Father. In order to fulfill the Father's will for Jesus to be "in all points tempted like as we are" (Hebrews 4:15 KJV), Jesus had to face these temptations without the benefit of any visual aids reminding Him of His very reason for being on the earth, of his Sonship, and of the Father's pre-earth ordinance (1 Peter 1:19–20 KJV). This separation would help enable the full extent of the human plight and struggle to be effectively realized in Jesus so He would not only qualify as Savior and Redeemer but would also make way for the fulfillment of our Lord's prophesied identity as empathetic Wonderful Counselor (Isaiah 9:6 KJV) and Righteous Judge (Isaiah 11:2, 4–5; 2 Timothy 4:1, 8 KJV).

Isolation of the Wilderness

The Savior's experience of the full effects of these temptations, both physical and mental, was then necessary. Jesus, being isolated and virtually blinded in the wilderness from the objects of His Love and mission, was required. Considering Jesus' great love for man (John 3:16, 15:13 KJV), the mere sight of a person would immediately engage that agape (supreme and unconditional) love of God the Father that flowed through Jesus' heart (John 15:1, 9, 17:23, 26 KJV). This would have served as instant inspirational aid in enduring any and all things. Jesus remained obedient to God the Father, enduring and overcoming in each of man's sorrows and struggles, trials and temptations without any visual motivational cues or stimuli. Isolation from Jesus' disciples and friends is likely one of the main reasons God the Father sent Jesus into the wilderness to endure His trials. Jesus' mind and body needed to be in about as strained a state as any person could be so He could be definitively tempted "in all points" or in all possible manners. God required the intensity of the effect of these temptations to be turned up to the maximum strength a human being could bear, hence both the isolation and in part, the forty-day fast prior to the temptation.

Sonship Shield and Identity

God the Father clearly had reason for telling Jesus to embark on this forty-day fast upon entering the wilderness for His temptation trials. As it turns out, the Devil's wilderness territory served to cloak the physical evidence of divine sonship from Jesus. There was the obvious visual shield created by the wilderness itself that prevented Jesus from seeing the manifestations of His Sonship in the lives of the disciples.

The prophet Isaiah also reveals through one of his prophetic declarations that the wilderness is the spiritual domain of Satan (Isaiah 34:13–17 KJV). Think of the wilderness as the opposite of the Garden of Eden. In the garden, God created the blessing for Adam to use to spread the beauty and the sweatless ease of the blessing from Eden throughout the whole Earth, and likely beyond (Genesis 1:22, 26, 28–30, 2:7–20 KJV). When Satan and his offspring, sin, stole the blessing, the blessing became a curse, which in turn covered the entire earth with thorns and briars (Genesis 3:17–18 KJV). The earth then becomes the wilderness (Isaiah 14:17 KJV), all except for the actual Garden of Eden, which God sealed off from fallen humanity and from Satan by hiding it and putting a cherub and a rotating, flaming sword to guard the entrance (Genesis 3:19 KJV).

After Adam sinned and the Earth fell into the hands of the Devil, Satan began to set up his kingdom, including principalities, rulers of the darkness, and spiritual wickedness in heavenly places or the skies—the atmosphere (Eph. 6:12 KJV). Satan is also called the Prince of the Power of the Air (Ephesians 2:2 KJV) and the god of this world, or age (2 Corinthians 4:4 KJV). The whole earth is in fact under the deception of the Devil's devious charms (Revelation 12:9 KJV). When God the Father instructed the Holy Spirit to lead Jesus into the wilderness, He was not simply referring to the world, which had become the wilderness, but into the midst of Satan's domain. This place is where Jesus would endure His trials, a concentration of the worst part of the earth, the darkest of the darkness, the wilderness of the wilderness. Here the Lord would endure some of the greatest temptations.

God, in His divine wisdom, was actually using Satan's temptations for His own purpose (Romans 8:28 KJV). The Devil's temptations could not have penetrated the mind of a readily Sonship-conscious Jesus. The Bible says Jesus did endure temptation, or in other words was in fact tempted. God the Father's will for Jesus to be tempted in all points like we are tempted called for the Lord's Sonship perception to be hampered.

How many Christians today are walking around not realizing their sonship relationship with God? Most Christians will profess they are sons of God even if they are still children of God maturing towards the faith place where they develop into sons and daughters. Calling oneself a son of God and actually *realizing* that sonship in the lives of the lost, with all the divine authority and miracle-working power sonship entails, are two very different things. Jesus said in Luke 6:44 that you will know them by their fruit, He didn't say by their words. "…each tree is recognized by its own fruit. People do not pick figs from thornbushes, or grapes from briars" (Luke 6:44 KJV). Remember what happened to the fig tree which bared no fruit in Mark 11:12-14, 20-26 KJV? The Apostle Paul said in 1 Corinthians 4:20 that "the kingdom of God is not in word but in power". It is only through the Holy Spirit–given revelation of our sonship with God in Christ, and God's power made available through that relation, that we through redemption have been given the ability to walk in the same divine authority, glory, and kingdom power Jesus had while on the earth (John 17:22 KJV). Yet even though God has given and made available His divine authority and power to all believers, it is not automatic, particularly when believers face continual temptations to doubt that sonship—thanks to the Devil's ploys.

Satan is considered the god of this world, or of this age, but as the prophet Isaiah revealed, this wilderness was both literally and symbolically a particularly heinous and evil place with evil spiritual predominance. The only way Satan could have had any effect at tempting Jesus is if there was a reason for Jesus to doubt His Sonship. At this very pivotal instant, God the Father's intent was revealed and Jesus proved yet again why the Father was so well pleased in Him. When Jesus was faced with no sensory evidence or conscious reminders of His Sonship, He revealed how to overcome the temptation to doubt. In the face of contradicting facts and very persuasive physical evidence, Jesus remained steadfastly connected spiritually to His Sonship through faith.

Jesus' divine Sonship as a full human, and the reality of the dispensation of grace, power, and authority intrinsically associated with a believer's identity of sonship with God the Father through faith, instantly eliminated the possibility of Satan's temptation having any lasting and fruitful effect on Jesus. The Messiah overcomes!

A likely reason God the Father had Jesus enter into the forty-day fast upon entering the wilderness for His trial was to exercise and build up Jesus' faith in His Sonship beyond what was seen or felt. This was so when the pressure of Satan's temptation came and Jesus was away from all friends and disciples, alone in those demon-infested woods, where it seemed there was no evidence of His Sonship, no miracle to remind Him, then Jesus would have to remain connected to His relationship with God through faith. Jesus' faith would be the evidence of things not seen from within the wilderness. The stamina in Spirit and faith Jesus accessed throughout His life and ministry was developed and strengthened by proper fasting and prayer, and He heavily relied upon it while enduring the test of this great trial in the wilderness.

Kingdom Nourishment for Spiritual Growth

SECOND COURSE
FASTING AND PRAYER

The revelation of spiritual preparation with fasting and prayer and meditating on God's Word for faith building is indeed a gift from God. It applies to all believers who will at some point come under trials, who are faced with temptations to doubt, and who come under other attacks of the Enemy. As the Devil tries to get the believer's mind to focus on the apparent natural or carnal situations which they can see evidence of through their eyes, believers must remember that any afflicting evidence hindering their health, their blessing and ultimately the will of God in their lives *is not* the truth of God's Word. Remember, Satan is the Deceiver of the whole world. He's a liar and a very good one, apparently.

As the believer increasingly learns to walk by faith and not by sight, the eyes of faith must grow keen and develop to distinguish the truth of God's eternal Word from the temporal illusion of physical evidence. This gives God the avenue to use His love power through the believer's unwavering faith to supernaturally change that natural fact into the everlasting truth of His word. As Moses describes in Genesis 1:26 KJV, God didn't let Adam and Eve borrow dominion of the earth, God decreed *let them have* dominion. Since God gave dominion and lordship of the earth to Adam (Genesis 2:15-23 KJV), the Father by His own righteousness and faithfulness cannot simply overstep His established law to change things, nor would He want to. For even God abides by His own laws. Therefore the believer must exercise the eyes of faith so God can work His will through them in the earth, even as He does in heaven, in agreement with His law. Through that unwavering faith in God, all things are indeed possible to him who believes. This steadfast faith is how believers avail themselves to God as conduits through which He can funnel His agape love and into whom God can impart the full measures of His power to manifest His will, His kingdom in all kinds of supernatural miracles for the deliverance of people.

"You shall know the truth, and the truth shall make you free" (John 8:32 KJV). The awareness of believers' true nature in Christ as co-laborers with God the Father (1 Corinthians 3:19 KJV), miracle-working sons and daughters and coheirs of God in Christ Jesus, must be shored up in faith with prayer and fasting and a close walk with God, and renewing the mind by meditating on His Word day and night (Ephesians 1:3–14, 3:8 KJV). Then God is able to manifest His *dunamis* creative, resurrecting, healing, demon-casting power through us without concern for a selfish misusing and abusing of that power. Jesus' victorious navigation through His trials in the wilderness, both physical and mental, were to be pictures for His disciples and for us to follow in the navigation of our lives and ministry. We all have a ministry, whether it be behind a pulpit in a church or synagogue, in the home caring for the family, at the head of a classroom, at the office in your cubicle, in the court house, the operating room, in the news room or on the beat protecting and serving. Wherever God calls us to be, we are to be ministers of God's love to the lost, and examples of true kingdom of God living, just like Jesus was.

Considering Jesus spent the majority of His life and ministry revealing to His disciples how to successfully live His abundant life (Matthew 11:27–30 KJV) and showing them how to overcome life's greatest trials (John 16:33 KJV), surely fasting and prayer was a premier and major lesson (Matthew 6:16 KJV). The Lord intended all of His disciples to follow Him and imitate Him both in acts of spiritual preparation for life's greatest moments of truth with fasting and prayer as well as to physically follow Jesus, to observe His effective methods and principles of ministry, learning (observing) to do them (Joshua 1:7; Nehemiah 1:5; Isaiah 1:18–19, 30:21, 55:2, Matthew 4:17, 19 KJV).

In fact, the act of fasting has been prevalent throughout the Hebrew culture for centuries and even today is present in many cultures and various religious practices. Fasting was also seen in the lives and ministries of the Pharisees of the Lord's day, albeit their methods were what Jesus revealed to be self-serving and unholy at best (Matthew 6:16 KJV). While they did lend themselves to the practice, in their case the act of fasting was to draw attention to themselves and was without proper reverence to maintain virtue in the conduct of it (Isa. 58:5 KJV). Still, the Pharisees' and Sadducees' observance of fasting serves to reveal some awareness of the importance of the practice in Hebrew culture. Therefore, one can deduce without much opposition that Jesus, being raised in the Hebrew culture of Nazareth, likely initially learned the practice of fasting from His parents as a boy and learned more of its history and cultural practice from His teachers and spiritual guides. Undoubtedly Jesus learned the most about His own significance in the observance of fasting from His heavenly Father (Matthew 9:14–16 KJV).

Luke, the physician disciple, tells us in his gospel account in chapter 2 and verses 36 through 40 of an eighty-four-year-old Aser tribe prophetess, Anna, who was married for seven years and widowed for sixty-four years and who never left from the temple of Jerusalem. Anna, Dr. Luke describes, served God with fasting and prayer night and day. She told everyone who came to the temple in Jerusalem seeking redemption about this boy Jesus whom she had finally met when Joseph and Mary came to the temple to pray and honor God by presenting baby Jesus in dedication to God the Father, Yahweh, as per Jewish custom. Anna, along with Simeon, was among the only believers convinced of the Savior's birth without having been told by people or actually having physically seen Jesus. While the wise men read the stars and believed, Anna may have been among the first to believe by faith through the word of the Spirit of God. This revealed word she would have received of the Spirit of God through fasting and praying (Matt. 16:17 KJV).

Surely Jesus had heard, among all His lessons, the story of the Prophetess Anna, who had blessed him as a baby and proclaimed the arrival of the Messiah. Learning the legend of her faithful devotions likely provided Jesus with additional insight and wisdom that would have a lasting impact on Jesus' walk and ministry, including His fasting and prayer life.

Proper Divine Order Revealed

Jesus' forty-day fast in the wilderness and the completion of the fast by the beginning of the Devil's temptations (Matthew 4:2–3 KJV) conveys it was likely a preparatory fast providing spiritual strength to endure the trials. However, one must also consider the reality of the physical toll on the body a forty-day fast has, which certainly would have intensified the effects of Satan's temptations. This physical effect may also be a reason for God calling Jesus to fast before the trial as the intent of these and all of Jesus' temptations was to endure the limits of or "all points" of the trials of our human plight. Jesus' fast was ultimately in obedience to God the Father in the fulfillment of His will and ordinance here in the earth.

In His fast, Jesus revered and honored God the Father, YHWH, as did every Jew and Christian dating back even to Moses, who instructed an unleavened bread fast as he described in his writing of Exodus 13:1–7 KJV. Fasting in reverence to God the Father was appropriate even for men during Moses' time. However, as the gospels reveal through Jesus' explanation to the Pharisees and to some followers of John the Baptist, Jesus Himself was now to be the object of Jesus' disciples fast and of believers' fasts. Why were the disciples not being allowed to continue fasting, paying homage to God the Father in heaven, while Jesus was among them? Why not allow the disciples to fast and pray to the Father *in addition to* seeking Jesus after His earthly departure to the Father? That would have been both redundant and erroneous, according to John 14:7–11 and 17:21 KJV. No one can separate Jesus from His Father. Honoring Jesus is, in fact, honoring the Father. One cannot honor the Father without honoring Jesus because no one comes unto the Father but through Jesus. He is the Door (John 10:9, 14:6 KJV).

A further examination of the details of Moses' fast reveals that even the objects of the fast in Exodus 13:1–7 KJV, including the unleavened bread, together with the circumstances of the sacrifices as ordered by God in verse 2, the firstborn males, human and animal, and "whatsoever openeth the womb among the children of Israel …" unlocks the mystery. The children of Israel being ushered by God through Moses out of the slavery of Egypt into the prosperous land of Canaan and into the land God promised them foreshadowed Jesus, the firstborn Son of God, ushering the church, believers, out of Satan's Babylonian faithless and prideful system of bondage to sin and into the selfless love and freedom of the kingdom of God and the promised heaven. The children of Israel went through a forty-year faith-proving wilderness (desert), where many fell by the way and only a few faithful endured (Hebrews 3:15–19 KJV) because of their close love walk with God. Jesus was also showing the disciples how walking in a close relationship on one accord with the Father with fasting and praying would also help them to overcome their wilderness temptations and trials of life, enabling them to be ushered by the Spirit of God into kingdom life more abundantly (John 10:10).

Fully aware of the true significance of the fast and understanding the revelation of His central role in the purpose of the practice, Jesus, in suspending all fasting by His disciples during His earthly mission (Matthew 9:14–17 KJV), also revealed to the disciples and to believers with ears of hearing the error of fasting in reverence to Jehovah God, while Jesus walked the earth. Many of the religious leaders and Pharisees erred in this manner. Some even today fast with their eyes on things other than what they should be on: the Lord Jesus Christ. Some, for instance, fast to get God to bless their wants more quickly instead of seeking to be divorced from earthly, worldly attachments and follow Jesus in walking closer with God by a more keen and discerning spirit. Regular fasting and praying with meditations on the truth of God's word helps position us to hear more clearly from God as we desperately yearn in love for Jesus' return and the rapture of the church.

Jesus illuminated the virtue that for His followers—for all believers—the fast is to be in reverence to Jesus Himself. Thereby the Lord categorically asserted both His ultimate divinity as well as God the Father's divine order. Since He was now in the earth, why would the disciples fast and yearn for the presence of God when God was literally in the flesh eating at the dinner table with them? Jesus' own fast was still in reverence to the Father, no doubt yearning for a return to the closeness He had with the Father from before the world was (John 17:5 KJV). In distinct heavenly order ("Thy will be done in earth, as it is in heaven"), the disciples were properly reserving their practice of fasting while Jesus remained in their midst and would resume fasting for Jesus after His death, burial, and resurrection. Then, as they resumed fasting, they would have been given and would follow the Holy Spirit, yearning for the Lord, even as we today follow the Fathers will by the leading of the Holy Spirit as we yearn for Jesus in our fasts looking forward to His second coming in power and glory (Matthew 9:14–17; Mark 2:18–22, 13:10-11, Luke 24:49, John 20:21-22, Acts 1:4-8 KJV).

Proper Humanity Order Revealed

A continuous fasting and prayer lifestyle helped Jesus the Christ to maintain, through faith, His close, intimate vertical connection with the Father in Spirit and in truth. Jesus said God the Father seeks such to worship Him, and it is by the Lord's same model that believers connect with the heavenly Father's will today (John 4:24 KJV). By engaging in daily, continuous meditation on God the Father's written (in the bible) and sent or proceeded word (delivered by the Holy Spirit or via angels or even via men of God inspired by the Holy Ghost) and maintaining an unyielding perpetual lifestyle of fervent prayer and regular and proper fasting, we receive the revelation of continually divorcing ourselves from the love of the world and the carnal desires of our flesh. We actively yearn for Jesus, the Living Word, in our fast just as Jesus yearned for the Father's face, seeking His will. Even as God longs to reveal Himself to us, we thereby can walk with Him even as Adam walked with God before the fall, and as Enoch walked with

God such that he was taken up, having finished his Earthly course to continue walking with God without passing through death. As Noah walked with God, and yes, even as the Lord Jesus Himself walked with the Father, believers today can follow Jesus' example, learning to walk in humble obedience to God, our Father as well.

Fasting and meditative prayer also keeps our minds and our physical bodies of flesh subservient to our spirits, which is the means God has provided us with in accessing synergy with God the Father in our walk with Him. Meditation on God's word continually renews our minds to the rhema truths God has embedded in His written word, the Holy Bible, and reveals those truths to our yielded spirits. As believers decisively chose to be lead with our spirits firmly engaged in lockstep with the direction of Holy Spirit for the completing of the Father's will, compelling our minds to follow our spirits and our bodies to then follow our minds, we properly align ourselves for God to do wonderful, mighty works in and through us. This is how believers can enter into our true dominion calling and kingdom purpose for which we were fearfully and wonderfully made (Psalm 139:14 KJV).

We know from Scripture about Jesus' very strong fasting and prayer lifestyle, and one can plainly see the evidence in Jesus' ministry from the many mighty miracles done at will. At whose will were Jesus' miracles done? At Jesus' will. Why? Not because Jesus was God, as Jesus never once touched His divinity scepter while walking this earth as a man, even though it remained the Lord's property the whole time (in God the Father's reserve, so to speak). Miracles were done at Jesus' will only and exactly because

Jesus' will and His words and actions were decisively in complete lockstep with the Father's ultimate and immediate will. Jesus never stepped outside the will of the Father, so Jesus' will and the Father's will were one in the same at all times (John 10:30 KJV). It was this uncompromising walk of Jesus, in full lockstep with God the Father that allowed God to trust Jesus with the full expression of His grace, including placing full creative power into the controlling hand or power of Jesus' faithful tongue.

God is also able to make *all* grace abound toward you, that ye *always*, having *all* sufficiency in *all* things may abound to *every* good work (2 Corinthians 9:8 KJV). Not only is God able, but that is also exactly what He wants to do. This desire comes directly out of the Father's supreme parental agape love for us, His children. Of course He wants to make *all* grace abound toward us, just like He did with Jesus when the Lord walked the earth … just like He did when Adam walked with God in the Garden of Eden before the fall. However, our Father will not hand over the keys to the brand new cherry-red, drop-top, tricked-out racing corvette to His children while we are the spiritual equivalent of raw, immature fourteen-year-old kids! He knows we would destroy ourselves and everyone around us if He gave that kind of power to us while we weren't ready for it. That doesn't mean *all* grace isn't ours even now. The corvette was made for us. We simply must faithfully (nothing wavering) allow God to spiritually mature us. We must be willing and obedient to follow and observe to do the preparative work as presented to us in the voluntary submissions of Jesus (Luke 2:40, 52; Hebrews 5:8–9 KJV). Then the Potter can begin to mold us into the mature anointed believers and skilled kingdom of God racecar drivers the Father created us and formed us in Christ to become (James 1:2–17; Ephesians 1:4 KJV).

Throughout the Lord's earthly life and ministry, every word Jesus ever said came directly from God the Father and through the Holy Spirit. So it was just like God Himself was on the earth subduing and reigning in full authority and power—just as God the Father intended it to be with mankind from the very beginning, starting with Adam in the garden. God revealed this synergy relation as the human believer faithfully operating in the power of God. God intends to abound the grace of His blessing in and through all believers who fully submit their will to God's will and who choose to lead uncompromising lives, walking by faith in the redemptive work and the Lordship of Jesus the Christ of Nazareth and in lockstep with the Holy Spirit of Truth, obedient to the word of God. As God's anointed believers who have been perfected in Christ through Jesus' finished work on the cross, Christians are to reign in the full dominion and the full authoritative power of God, just like Jesus and pre-fall Adam. For this manifestation, we are not waiting on God; God is waiting on the Church, the body of worldwide believers to faithfully march together on one accord (Act 2:1 KJV) with kingdom purpose, living by and preaching Jesus' life more abundantly (John 10:10 KJV), which God has set before us!

Copycat

Very early on in Jesus' ministry, this will synergy training between God the Father and Jesus can be seen emerging, and it was revealed even as far back as when Jesus was a boy of twelve years of age. Back when Jesus absconded from Mary and Joseph for about five days, rendering the clueless parents desperate, they began to retrace their steps from where they had traveled, a day's journey toward Galilee, back to where they had been in Jerusalem. They continued searching throughout the holy city for three days, looking for their precious boy. Then on the third day of searching Jerusalem, Mary and Joseph found Jesus in the temple ministering to and astonishing even the doctors who heard Him speak. This was incidentally a clear foreshadowing of the three-day period the world would "lose" Jesus after Calvary, before His triumphant resurrection and reappearance to minister and serve as victorious intercessor and redeemer. The Lord would once again astonish everyone with His continuing miracle-working ministry, as it now would be performed through His disciples and today through faithful believers (John 14:12–13 KJV).

The Bible says in Luke 2:48 KJV that Mary and Joseph finally reached Jesus in the temple of Jerusalem. The manner in which little twelve-year-old Jesus replied to them as they implored why He, in their minds, had disrespected His parents by getting lost and staying lost for five total days without even looking for them or attempting to contact them stunned Mary and Joseph. They weren't quite ready for Jesus's matter-of-fact tone which undoubtedly shocked them. Therefore the parents did not fully realize the deep truth behind little Jesus' reply. Luke 2:49 KJV says, "And He said unto them, 'How is it that ye sought me? wist ye not that I must be about my Father's business?'" Jesus' response reveals both His already strong fasting life, going five days without food at twelve years old, and His seeking lockstep connection to the will of Jesus' true Father, Jehovah God in heaven, even to the seeming disregard of His earthly parents.

Of course, it is possible that strangers may have attempted to feed little twelve-year-old Jesus during His five days of ministering. The Bible doesn't reveal this definitively one way or the other. It is unlikely, however, that Jesus would have accepted, given the stark parallel of Jesus' own words later when Jesus' disciples tried to feed him in John 4:31–34 KJV and Jesus replied, "I have meat that ye know not of ... My meat is to do the will of Him that sent me, and to finish His work." Luke 2:52 KJV also confirms that the boy-king Jesus grew and matured, increasing in wisdom and stature, and in favor with God and man.

It should be noted that Jesus never disobeyed His earthly parents, as revealed in Scripture, unless unbeknownst to Mary and Joseph, their request directly contradicted the will of Jesus' heavenly Father. Clearly Jesus' parents would never intentionally ask Jesus to do anything outside of God's will, as they themselves were obedient and faithful people (Luke 1).

Spiritual Dominion

Clearly the Holy Spirit's leading of Jesus into the wilderness to fast and pray and to be tempted of Satan was not Jesus' introduction to the concept of fasting and praying. Therefore, we can know from His walk with the Father that as Jesus led an active and fervent fasting and prayer lifestyle, He probably did not enjoy excessive amounts of bodily, fleshy reserves to nutritionally draw from upon entering into this forty-day fast. It might be argued that God the Father could have revealed to Jesus that He would be fasting and not eating for nearly a month and a half several weeks in advance, giving Jesus an opportunity to eat more and "plump up" in preparation. But that simply is not scriptural and is highly doubtful given the disciplined and obedient yet free lifestyle Jesus led. God the Father and the Holy Ghost were with Jesus in the wilderness, watching to keep Him sustained, as Jesus knew, and as we know primarily from God's Word where He says, "I will never leave you or forsake you" (Deuteronomy 31:6; Hebrews 13:5 KJV). We also know from the timely sending forth to Jesus of the ministering angels after He successfully overcame the Devil's temptations (Matthew 4:11; Mark 1:13 KJV).

It is also guaranteed that zero Holy Ghost anesthetic was used during this trial period to ease Jesus' suffering. Having to resist an all-out assault of Jesus' as yet greatest temptations by His mortal enemy, while enduring the starvation hunger pains of a forty-day fast, and alone in the wickedness of the wilderness, was the trial of the ages. The Holy Ghost helps us today get through our most difficult trials in His role as our Comforter and Counselor-Teacher, but Jesus' very purpose for enduring these temptations and trials was clearly illustrated by the apostle Paul in Hebrews 4:14–16 KJV to become our compassionate high priest.

For our sakes, Jesus was to be Himself tempted in all points as we are—tempted by the Devil, ultimately tempted by those close to Him, tempted even by His flesh and His own mind concerning

His reservations about His destiny, revealed explicitly during Jesus' struggle in the garden of Gethsemane. We can know that Jesus' endurance of all temptations, together with His complete and total overcoming of all of them by making the right choice in each situation, gives Him credence to be our sympathetic, empathetic, understanding, and ultra-compassionate Brother, Friend, Sustainer, Strong Tower, Deliverer, Healer, Redeemer, Sanctifier, Good Shepherd, Intercessor, Advocate, Light, Guide, Captain, King, Lord, Savior, and Author and Finisher of our faith.

Kingdom Nourishment for Spiritual Development

THIRD COURSE
PERSPECTIVE

In the wilderness of Matthew 4:1–11, Jesus also relented to several voluntary temptable submissions. The forty-day fast was one, as Jesus resisted the basic human survival reflex to consume food to avoid starvation. The Lord successfully resisted the survival reflexes to adjust circumstances as one is able to end those intense hunger pains. He also chose to submit to the long period of human solitude in the wilderness, foregoing the basic need for contact and communion with a species of like intellect. This need, or at least desire, is present even in God the Father, as evidenced by His very creation. God Himself is Love, yet as fully self-contained as God is, the full expression of God's love was not complete in only loving Himself, who was and is perfect (Luke 6:25–36 KJV).

The psychological human need to "feel" one is loved was also a voluntary submission that encompasses all of the other temptable submissions of Jesus. We again learn from Jesus' example to trust in God's love for us even when all natural evidence appears to be contrary. God said, "I will never leave you or forsake you." Learn to trust that. "Though you make your bed in hell, I am with you." Choose definitively to believe that. Trust in the Lord, and lean not on your own understanding. Decisively take and have more confidence in the infallible truth of God's eternal word than you have in carnality and in the temporal physical evidence of Babylon that Satan and Mammon use to try sway your trust. The truth of God's Word is that Satan's power and Babylon are destroyed completely by the Lord Jesus (1 John 3:8, John 17:4, 19:30 KJV). Only people's faith in the Devil, which Satan builds through lies and deception, and then accesses through the people's fear, worry, doubt, and apathy can resurrect him in their life. That is how powerful faith is. God says fear not those difficult, sometimes impossible circumstances in your life. Don't fear the Devil. Fear is perverted faith. Keep your faith in God so He and the eternal truth of His Word, Jesus, will be made manifest in your life. Don't even fear what looks and seems impossible. If God said it, believe it. God *flosses His teeth* with our perceived "impossible". Get the picture?

One might say, "Well, Jesus' submissions weren't really voluntary if the Holy Spirit led Jesus into the wilderness." While it is true that Jesus was led into the wilderness by the Spirit, as always, Jesus had a choice. It might appear as though Jesus didn't have a choice by the way He always responded so immediately the instant God's word was given to Him, but Jesus did in fact always have a choice. He was at all times during His thirty-two-year earthly experience one hundred percent human, in addition to being one hundred percent God. Just like all humans, Jesus had a will. By our will, we make our choices, both actively as well as passively by choosing not to act on certain things we know or believe or are told that we should. The fact of the matter is Jesus didn't ever wait until He was asked or told to do something by God the Father before He decided He would do it. We can observe in scripture and throughout the gospels that Jesus' successful walk with God is due in part to the fact that the Savior decided very early on that whatever God said, whatever Jesus was instructed to do by the Father, the Lord was doing it already or had already decided to do it at the appointed time long before the Devil even had an opportunity to try to swindle Him out of it. Take note of this; it can make your walk with God so much freer and less tumultuous, not having to deal with as many of Satan's attacks of doubt and what if this happens or that doesn't happen. You can cut most of Satan's temptation off at the pass just like Jesus did. Simply make up your mind beforehand. Make it up right now, this instant, that the answer is always "yes sir, Lord. Yes to whatever You ask of me, Heavenly Father. Even before You ask it, Abba, the answer is yes." Then, keep your word at all costs.

Spirit Led

Jesus, while human, always chose to follow the lead of the Spirit, who in turn always follows God's Word (John 16:13 KJV). Satan used the opportunity of this wilderness trial to set himself about to tempt Jesus in the very core, basic level of the Messiah's human existence. This temptation test was for Satan, the golden chance he had searched for all those years to disrupt the plan of God revealed in the garden (Genesis 3:15 KJV), and a window of opportunity had finally presented itself. According to the Devil's calculations, obtained from the culmination of ages of carefully observing and studying people from Adam and Eve to Joseph and Mary and their boy-king Jesus the Christ in desperate search for this prophesied seed of Eve who would bruise the head of the serpent, the most impressionable and persuadable aspect of the human psyche was the self-perception. This is precisely why it was Jesus' Sonship with God the Father, more specifically Jesus' perception of His Sonship, that Satan bet all of his chips and went all in on as being his best opportunity. The devil decided this was likely going to be his most advantageous go-for-broke, potential chink in the armor attack point of the Messiah.

Might this be the one area where the steadfast resolve of Jesus, the Son of man might budge, even just a smidgen? Jesus was, after all, in the midst of all the sufferings that combined to make up the intense pressure-cooker effect of this temptation trial. In the wilderness, the heart of the Devil's home territory, and during this opportunistic appointed season, Satan was crouched, ready to make his move against God. Satan ultimately wanted to hurt God by destroying his beloved mankind, even as he sought to preserve his own existence. Judging from the scriptures' account of his evil nature, Satan himself probably didn't even know whether he more greatly valued his plight for self-preservation or the innate, hateful rage that fueled his desire to hurt God by destroying mankind. In either case, success for Satan clearly had to go through this Messiah Jesus, and here He was, virtually served to him on a platter.

In His divine wisdom, God the Father had established in Jesus' person command of two natures, one was one hundred percent God as the second person of the Trinity, and the other one hundred percent human, the son of the virgin Mary and the seed of Eve. This wisdom afforded Jesus the opportunity to fulfill God the Father's word and plan by walking the earth fully as a human, tempted like as we are yet without sin, and without once touching His second person of the Trinity divine scepter at any point. The humanity in which Jesus was necessarily clothed, and that the Lord embraced and ultimately became, was commissioned by God the Father to conquer mankind's sin rebellion and to rectify the dying course of the world that Adam's sinful choice set in motion.

Sin, the manifested work of Satan that yields death as offspring, and the cursed-earth consequence thereof was to be forever swallowed up in the victory of the Messiah Savior's successfully fulfilled ordinance by God the Father. As Jesus, the Second Adam, succeeded in overcoming temptation to sin where the first Adam, God's first-formed son, failed, Jesus would become our willing sacrificial Lamb. Our righteousness, then, is accounted unto us not through faithful obedience as it was with Abraham and the old covenant fathers of the faith, but rather by confession through faith in the sacrificial redeeming shed blood of Jesus and His eternal Lordship. The obedience of today's born-again believer, who is made righteous by the blood of the Lamb, comes after redemption and sanctification and comes through our blood-bought, faith-imputed righteousness. We are faithful and obedient because of Jesus' righteousness which is gracefully imputed into us, not by any initial righteousness of our own will to obtain it. Our own will apart from the Lord is wicked and sinful *only*. The greatest news is that even today, believers in Jesus Christ are never apart from Lord (Deuteronomy 31:6, Hebrews 13:5 KJV).

As believers abide in the righteousness which was purchased by Jesus' sacrificial blood, (not earned through works) and as we stay in God's Word, keeping it in our eyes, our ears, and our mouths and on our minds and in the midst of our hearts constantly, we continue to grow in God's grace and faith. All attempts to be righteous and holy outside of Jesus' redemption are viewed as filthy rags by God because they lead to pride and self-exaltation. These are not of the kingdom of God; rather they are the hallmarks and badges of Satan's cursed kingdom of darkness and Babylon (Isaiah 64:6 KJV). They are the essence of Satan's own nature and are in fact what caused Satan to get booted from heaven. Only the grace imparted righteous works that we've done for God's kingdom, and in the name of Christ Jesus will stand the end-time test of fire (1 Corinthians 3:13–15 KJV).

The goal of the believer today must be in a sense to return this "sin-scorched" earth back to the state of the Garden of Eden in preparation for Jesus' glorious return in power and glory. We must realize the true nature of what Jesus' finished work on the cross did for us through redemption and once again accept God's assignment, and Jesus's commission to keep the earth as Adam kept the Garden of Eden by walking with God and enforcing through faith God's Way, Truth and Life (John 14:6 KJV). This is a manifestation of the prayer Jesus told His disciples to pray,

"Our Father which art in heaven, hallowed be thy name, Thy kingdom come, Thy will be done in Earth, as it is in heaven ..." (Matthew 6:9–10 KJV). The kingdom of heaven is inside of faithful believers as a seed which God planted. God's plan for Adam and for mankind was not abandoned when Adam sinned. Rather, God sent Jesus to fix and "answer" the sin problem so that we would be able to resume the "keeping" of the earth. Jesus' ministry was a perfect example of the "keeping of the earth" which comprises true kingdom living. This is the revelation of Mark 13:10 KJV that the gospel shall be published among all nations. Luke 21:31 KJV says that by this kingdom gospel publication and the ensuing persecutions, we know that the kingdom of God is nigh at hand. These signs and wonders and miracles are the evidence of the kingdom of God, they are the fruit of the Vine (Luke 22:18, Mark 14:25, Matthew 7:13-23 KJV).

This is also the revelation of Jesus' command and declaration (not suggestion) in John 14:12 KJV. "Verily, Verily I say unto you, He that believeth in Me, the works that I do shall he do also and greater works than these, because I go unto my Father." In the garden pre-fall, Adam was indeed effectually doing God's will in keeping the garden, and naming all of the species with full faith even as the angels in the kingdom of heaven do God's will with full faith. God made all animals and all of earthly creation subject to man's faith-filled word. (Eve was not even a little bit frightened by the talking dragon-serpent? There is nothing to be afraid of when all moving things are subject to your authority). God willed for pre-fall Adam to keep the garden and to spread the blessing of the garden with dominion over all the earth. After the first Adam failed, Jesus, the second Adam, was sent to redeem man's breech, and to successfully show us how kingdom living is to be done.

Adam sinned and failed, but even from before the world was, Jesus *is* the complete answer to all of what happened to man and to man's dominion when Adam sinned and handed it over to the devil. At the moment of the fall, Genesis 3:7 KJV says that the eyes of Adam and Eve were opened. Not that the couple had walked around the garden with their eyes shut bumping into the animals and trees and each other, but rather their carnal eyes of faith in what their senses told them were opened and preferred over their spiritual eyes of trusting God alone. The intoxication of pride then enveloped Adam and instead of trusting and preferring his pre-sin spiritual eyes which enabled him to walk by faith in synergy with God, Adam's new default way and vision was with his carnal and fleshy eyes. Adam switched from first trusting only in God's word and the resulting blessing and true kingdom living to now trusting what he physically saw and heard and tasted and felt. That false autonomy, stoked by Satan's lies, filled Adam with a killer sense of self and pride that set him on the course toward despising God and toiling through the thorns and briars barely making a living by the sweat of his brow (Genesis 3:17-19 KJV). Adam effectively handed his faith and thereby the keys of earth's dominion over to the Devil who left Adam and Eve to fin for themselves as soon as the Devil got what he wanted...dominion over the earth.

But God had a plan, seeing this part coming, and so He sent Jesus, who loved us and died for us even when we were still in our selfishness and sin. Jesus showed us through His life and ministry how to really love once again and how to walk by faith in God and once again "keep" the earth through God's love by seeking first the kingdom. It is by using the very power of God through faith to fulfill God's will for mankind which has never changed. God still wants us to have and enforce the dominion which Jesus came to restore. Jesus took care of the Devil and indeed destroyed the power of his dominion. Unfortunately, Satan has set up many tricks and deceptions to confuse people about the truth of his demise and peoples real destiny. People still believe the devil has authority over them. He does not. The only influence Satan has is that which people *give* the Devil through faith. When people fear the Devil, and when people choose to follow Satan's way of pride, selfishness, covetous lust and manipulation through lies, they are subscribing to and following the pillars of the kingdom of darkness. God said through the prophet Isaiah in chapter 54 verse 17 that no weapon formed against you shall prosper. If you really believe this, then you *cannot* fear Satan, because if God is for you, who can be against you?

Acts (The Works)

God, *by His Word*, made all natural and physical things including life itself (John 1:1-4 KJV). Jesus tried for three years of ministry to reveal the kingdom of God, kingdom of heaven life (obediently placed faith filled words creating) to the disciples. The Savior also worked to build up the disciples' own faith for the Kingdom work and the destiny which soon awaited them (Mark 9:19 KJV). After Jesus died and was risen, the disciples were finally able to fully digest the powerful reality of this awesome truth. The eternal superiority of God's word over the natural and physical was finally seen spiritually by each of the disciple through the eyes of their faith.

On one particular day each disciple attended a prayer and ministry meeting in the upper room of the synagogue during the Jewish celebration of Pentecost, a term which means the fullness of times and signifies the number of days since the Passover, which was fifty. The disciples and even their wives and sisters and daughters were all full of faith and in perfect agreement, praising God and praying in this spirit of truth, all on one accord like a large choir singing pitch-perfectly on every single note. This is when the Holy Spirit of God came and sat on each of them like fire. It was the fullness of time and God's creative power was once again released through man, just like Adam in the garden, and the disciples began to keep the earth by the power of God's Spirit, healing the sick and raising the dead. They were walking with God, believing that the Spirit of His holy Word is the Truth and final authority of what happens on earth, just like the operation of the kingdom of heaven. They did not believe that those things which they saw, sickness, poverty and death was "just the way things are". Those unfortunate occurrences, along with all "misfortunes" that happens to people are a direct result of people historically choosing like Adam chose in the Garden of Eden, to try to make it on their own without God. Listening to and believing the lies of the devil causes selfishness and pride to grow. When the disciples preached the truth revelation of the kingdom of God in the name of the crucified and risen Jesus Christ, they brought Light to those who were caught up in the lies of the devil and who were consequently so afflicted. Jesus had said to the disciples "the words that I speak to you, they are spirit and they are life". Jesus also said "I am the Way, the Truth and the Life…" The Holy Spirit revealed these Truths to the disciples and that truth made them free enough to follow in Jesus' footsteps going in the power of the Spirit healing the sick, raising the dead, casting out demons and effectively living and doing the kingdom of heaven acts while in the midst of this world. The devil tricked and lied and swindled most of the people of the world into going far away from God's plan. Jesus destroyed the works and the power of the devil. Now the disciples were keeping the earth, enforcing the truth of the devil's defeat and bringing the light and truth of Jesus to the world.

True dominion cannot be had with a billion dollars. One can perhaps try to fake it for a little while and deceive some people until the money runs out or whatever, but true dominion is done only through declaring and confidently speaking, in Jesus' name, those exact faith-filled words which are sent from God the Father and delivered to us by the Holy Spirit. Faith in what? Faith both in God's *ability* to do all good things for us and through us for others, as well as faith in God's divine parental *desire* to do all things through the faith of the believer who has been redeemed by the blood of the Lamb. We must once again learn to walk with God and trust more in the eternal truth of God's love, God's word, and in the reestablishment of the dominion which Jesus' finished work on the cross accomplished for those who truly live and walk by faith. True faith in God requires no longer trusting in the worldly illusions and temporal facts of this age, and then speaking out on those lies by saying things like "I'm sick" or "I just know I'm going to feel terrible tomorrow. I am catching the flu." Confirming that physically felt or seen natural fact with our words of faith is the dumbest thing we Christians do all the time! The facts of the beginning symptoms of sickness might be seen with the physical eye and felt in our body, but they are no less inferior to the truth of God's word which says we are healed by Jesus' stripes. Giving up hope and declaring defeat by speaking the words of the devil's lies with your faith-filled word, when God's word says you are healed by His stripes is not the will of God. Often times the doctor's report sounds and looks grim, but whose report will you believe, the doctor's or God's word? Realizing this concept indeed requires true repentance through submitting to the Holy Spirit and allowing Him to change our thinking. This is when bible studies and meditation on the truth of God's word helps us by renewing our minds (Romans 12:2 KJV).

The challenge for believers is to close the door of trust in the carnal eyes or the physical senses and begin to live and speak the truth of God's love in faith. Then believers will produce the miraculous 'abundant life' fruit of the kingdom of heaven which Jesus spoke of (Matthew 7:16-18, John 10:10 KJV), by allowing God to open and mature their spiritual eyes so they can see and understand God as He truly is. This fruit will then manifest both in the believer's life as well as in the lives of those around them, particularly in those who make Jesus their Lord also.

The necessary buildup of patience and faith is often a painful experience to the selfish and impatient flesh. All flesh seeks immediate gratification and it tries desperately to influence the mind. Every morning, believers must make a quality (not half-hearted) decision to die to that carnality, and to refuse the leadership of the flesh in our daily decisions. Then the Holy Spirit will help us by compelling the flesh to submit to our spirit which now desires to follow the Holy Spirit. You once were blind when you trusted the eyes of your flesh, but now, in Christ Jesus, you see truth with your heart.

The believer's full faith must from now on and forever be exclusively in the truth of God's Word. The believer's faith walk must remain fully in lockstep with the *invisible* Spirit of God despite what the fleshy eyes may visibly reveal, or whatever carnal temporal facts the flesh conveys. God the Holy Spirit then becomes our spirit's personal fitness trainer. As we nourish our spirit with the word, and the Holy Spirit trains us through progressive trials as faith weights in our lives, our spirit grows in us stronger than our flesh and our mind. Our faith filled words reflect the redemption Jesus paid for with His blood after Calvary, we reach new levels of life and dominion within God's will and plan. Jesus said in John 6:63 KJV that it is the spirit that gives life, the flesh profits nothing. The words that I speak to you, Jesus said, they are spirit and they are life.

Spoiled and Defeated Foe

God the Father sent Jesus into the world to destroy the deceptive misleading works of the Devil (1 John 3:8 KJV) and foreordained the Lord for this task even before the foundations of the world (1 Peter 1:20 KJV). Jesus also enforced God's superior word in truth over the temporal natural world including the lies and illusions of the Devil, temptation, sickness, bondage, poverty and lack, doubt, fear, and ultimately death. The life of Jesus reminds us of what God intends for man to do and why Jesus came to return those who would believe in Jesus as Lord, who are walking by faith and not by sight to the dominion status which God originally created man for. This is the revelation of Jesus sitting at the right hand of the Father until His enemy is placed under His feet (Psalm 110:1, Matthew 22:44 KJV). We the church are the body of Christ and Jesus is the Head. Jesus effectively destroyed the lies of the devil, and we must now walk out that victory with our blood-of-the-Lamb-purchased dominion and enforce the truth of God's eternal word. Then the smoke and mirror lies of the devil will come crashing down as people will begin to realize and receive the healing from sickness and freedom from bondage to sin that Jesus' finished work has already provided them.

As Jesus was foreordained for His redemptive mission even before "Let there be light", so were all believers also predestined in Jesus as victorious overcomers before creation, according to the Father's purpose (1 John 2:3; Ephesians 1:4 KJV). It is clear from Jesus' great cry for mercy in the garden of Gethsemane, followed immediately by total submission to God's will, that even He at times during his walk in a flesh suit struggled with the detailed foreknowledge of the torturous plight that awaited Him at the culmination of His ordained human destiny (Isaiah 53:3–5, 10–12; Matthew 26:39; Mark 14:36; Luke 22:42 KJV). What followed is the same thing that followed whenever Jesus was tempted. Jesus' flesh succumbed to His Spirit which was firmly engaged in lock-step with the will of God the Father. Not my will but Thy will, oh Lord, be done. God's way may "look" tougher, but it is far better than the flesh-serving way we might contrive which might appear easier or more immediately gratifying but is ultimately ill-fated.

Kingdom Nourishment for Spiritual Development

FOURTH COURSE
KNOW YOUR ENEMY

The Devil knew Jesus was the key to mankind's redemption from the cursed effects Satan had managed to accomplish through the serpent in the Garden of Eden with Adam and Eve. Having been foretold by God Himself of the Messiah's prophetic mission to destroy Satan and the kingdom Satan would erect out of that successful seduction in the garden, the Devil studied mankind for many generations as he searched for this Messiah to come. From all of the psychological information amassed, Satan has learned what tempts humans. Satan, The Opposer, may well be assisted in the strategic manipulation of the knowledge of what tempts man by the Devil's own deviousness and charmed deceptiveness. However, all anyone really has to do to know your temptations is to simply hang around you for a while. Your behavior reveals all anyone needs to know concerning your carnal weaknesses. Even that spider up in the corner of your bedroom knows your sinful temptations. Since the Devil is neither omniscient nor omnipresent, the way he has been watching and observing us our whole lives is through his demonic spy spirits.

For those of you reading this who are currently making a mental note to pick up a can of Raid and a cobweb duster on your next trip to the store, that might not be a bad idea. Remember though, we wrestle not with flesh and blood but with principalities, spiritual wickedness in high places, and rulers of the darkness of this world. So keeping your full godly armor on and *using it* keeps you safe and spiritually effective (Ephesians 6:10–18 KJV).

Evil spy demons watch and report back to Satan, and you better believe Satan has a file on you, particularly if you are a born-again believer (Ephesians 6:12 KJV). As soon as you make that confession that Jesus is your Lord, you shoot right to the top of the Devil's interest pile because you now are headed in the direction of God's will which is to enforce by faith the Truth of Jesus' thorough defeat of the devil, helping others to know the truth as well. Now, when Satan gets wind of your receiving revelation of the true nature of your sonship, you immediately become top priority enemy number one! When born-again believers truly awaken to the full reality of their sonship through faith in the redeeming shed blood of Jesus the Lamb of God and what exactly that redemption really means, the Holy Spirit begins to cultivate and mature the comprehension and full conceptualization of all the authority which divine sonship entails.

That God-ordained authority, when exercised in truth and light by spiritually aware sons and daughters of God, lends itself to believers accurately and with understanding wielding God almighty's universe-creating, Messiah-resurrecting, angel-commanding, Holy Spirit–synergizing, dunamis power which is enacted by faithfully and obediently speaking God's Word as led by His Spirit. This divine authority wielding process is seen repeatedly throughout the ministry of Jesus and His disciples as Jesus worked tirelessly to convince the disciples that their power lies not in the seen, but in faith of the superiority of unseen Spirit, the life of the word of the kingdom of God. The Devil's kingdom of darkness with its lies and temptations then have zero effect because Satan the Trickster doesn't stand a chance against people who faithfully resist him with the light of truth, so he flees (Matthew 4:11, James 4:7 KJV). How effective would David Copperfield, Chris Angel and other professional illusionists be if their smoke and mirror stunts were revealed by light and clarity? So even the Father of Lies cannot operate where there is revelation of truth and light.

With God's power in our faithfully obedient authoritative hands, we can take right up where our brother and Lord King Jesus left off by spiritually administering and enforcing the truth of the total defeat of the Devil. Remember, Jesus has already won that victory, and Satan was made a spoiled and thoroughly defeated foe two thousand years ago on the first Easter Sunday (Colossians 2:15 KJV). Satan's only influence today comes from the fear and doubt he is able to swindle and bully into the confused minds of people who don't realize it's just a lie and an illusion. Satan has already been whipped, stripped naked, and left quivering in the floor of the pit of hell in front of all of the cohorts of the region of the damned when Jesus took back the keys to death, hell and the grave (Colossians 2:15, Revelation 1:18 KJV).

Now, it is never wise to underestimate the Devil or to be ignorant of his devices. Jesus continuously overcame sin and temptation by being shored up with faith to overcome. Maintaining a perpetually close walk with the Father through constant prayer, regular fasting, and abiding in God's Word is how Jesus' faith kept Him steps ahead of the Devil's schemes and attacks. Satan, however, displayed some insight into Jesus' struggles, which he could have gotten even if he relied solely on the psychological history of mankind. Satan has always known God and the Son of God as all powerful. In fact, that power is what he coveted when he was the angel Lucifer (Isaiah 14:14 KJV). However, Satan also knew that during this wilderness confrontation with Jesus, in this particular moment in time Jesus was in fact required to be fully a man. The Devil also knew from God's decree in the Garden of Eden in Genesis 3:15 KJV of the Messiah to come being the seed of a woman that because of His destiny, Jesus was not allowed to assume His role as divine Son and second person of the Trinity at any time during His human experience or He'd be *immediately disqualified* as the seed of Eve. The seed of Eve could not directly exhibit any divine power of his own will, outside God the Father's will, because the seed of Eve means human. Humans cannot exhibit or use God's divine power outside of God's will. If Jesus tried to stay walking on the water longer than He was supposed to and outside of God's will, the Lord would have sunk like a rock. As Jesus Himself said, it was never Jesus that did the works as Jesus walked the earth, but it was the Father inside of Jesus who produced the power by His Holy Spirit and did the works (John 14:10 KJV).

Now Jesus, who had witnessed the Devil's original transformation from the angel Lucifer (Luke 10:18; Isaiah 14:12 KJV) and subsequent fall from grace like lightning to the Earth, called out Satan's motivation and his mission, which has never changed. In John 10:10 KJV Jesus said "The thief cometh not but for to steal, and to kill and to destroy …" So in order to effectively steal, kill, and destroy God's cherished mankind, the Devil had to study this being, man. And study him Satan did, for thousands of years as he scoured the globe with murderous intent directed at the Messiah, the seed of woman, which would bruise his head (Genesis 3:15 KJV).

The motivation of Satan's study of the human race was twofold. The Devil's intense observations were motivated by his futile desire for self-preservation and the consequential need to seek out and destroy that Messianic seed, before it could destroy him and all his evil works. That motive was coupled with Satan's blinding rage toward humankind and his accompanying ambition to destroy those very objects of God's love.

This theme of kingdom rulers seeking to prematurely and permanently terminate any potential threats that could arise to overthrow the ruler has pervaded throughout the authoritarian history of mankind. Here Satan displays sinister authorship of this tactic. Both Satan's knowledge of Scripture as well as the personal prophecy given directly to him from the very mouth of God the

Father in the Garden of Eden upon being cursed for deceiving mankind (Genesis 3:15 KJV) revealed for the Devil a pretty bleak story. However, the prophetic word from God the Father did manage to make Satan privy to a more profound reality.

Satan heard God decree that this anointed Savior of man would be a seed of Eve (i.e., human). The Devil knew from personal experience that although God is supremely loving, even He is legally bound by His own holy, righteous judgment. In other words, God Himself cannot overstep His own law even to display the love and mercy He so longs to. That is why God couldn't let Adam and Eve stay in the Garden after they broke His law and sinned notwithstanding God's love toward them, which was no less after the first 'first family' sinned than before. They broke God's law first in their minds with help of the Deceiver, then in their hearts, and finally with their bodies. And as God warned Adam in Genesis 2:17 KJV, the wages of sin (willful disobedience) is death (Romans 6:23 KJV). Sin and its offspring death, separation from God, crippled the man, and Satan watched as God banished His beloved mankind from the garden. It is the heart of man that God is after.

If a man's heart through confession chooses God, truly repents from selfishness and love of the carnal world, and instead seeks the Lord Jesus earnestly, then even if sin happens in his flesh, that man's heart becomes saddened and disgusted by it, but the man is eternally saved and washed clean from all sin. He has been forgiven and the Holy Spirit's shame and conviction to do better does not in truth become condemnation over what has been done.

God's law still required all of mankind to suffer the penalty of God's wrath for Adam's epic blunder. The Bible says God knows the end from the beginning, so even before God began to create the universe, God knew Adam would flunk this test. That is why Jesus was foreordained before the foundations of the world to be our Savior, the second Adam, who would be a human, like Adam, but this time would fully pass the test and keep God's law throughout His entire human destiny.

In God's divine wisdom, His plan, which was in place even before the earth was formed, was to send into the earth of Himself the Son, the actual second person of the Trinity, the Triune God, to pass through Eve's womb via Mary as the only humanly begotten Son of God the Father (John 3:16 KJV). Thereby Jesus, the anointed Son of God, became a human who fulfilled God's law in its entirety by living fully as a human and never sinning but rather overcoming sin. When faced with temptation to sin, Jesus made the right decision every single time throughout His entire life and so He fulfilled, as was prophesied, all of the holy, priestly sacrifices of spotless lambs and goats throughout all the ages of old.

Those sacrifices were all a part of the plan and will of God the Father, as they were to foreshadow the ultimate redeeming sacrifice through the shedding of the blood of Jesus, the final spotless, sinless Lamb of God (Hebrews 9:22 KJV). Unlike mankind, Satan and the angels that fell with him are not so lucky for their Judas betrayal of the Father. After having been in the very heavens with God and a part of all the holiness therein, their sin constituted an unpardonable and unforgivable breach. However evil and stupidly ambitious Satan is, he is still clever, as that is how God originally made him as Lucifer the general of the musical hosts of heaven before he went rogue (Isaiah 14:11-12 KJV). He did not miss the revelation of mankind's Savior having to be a human man and coming through the seed of Eve as God decreed. The Devil was surely not going to take defeat lying down. Ultimately, however, his fate and the fate of all his cohorts are sealed, as Revelation 20:10 KJV proclaims.

Jesus in Satan's Cross-Hairs

The Bible says Jesus was led up by the Spirit into the wilderness to be tempted, so Jesus was actually mentally and physically tempted. In fact, during His temptation, Jesus was just nearing the end of His forty-day fast, so His mind and body were also most likely weakened by intense physical hunger after not eating for so long. This would cause the effect of the temptation to have even greater impact. With Jesus' mind and body in this physically strained state, and Satan knowing at this point who the Messiah was, the Devil surely prepared the most conniving and clever and the most insidious and crafty temptations he could possibly muster. And it was all tailored and designed specifically, exclusively to entice one person: the Redeemer.

Satan still had in mind his success in tempting the first Adam in the Garden of Eden. Surely the success of that endeavor played a key role in the planning process for the temptation of this second Adam. How did Satan succeed the first time? He went through the one Adam loved: his wife, Eve. Notice though in the wilderness, that Satan did not use people as bait, tempting Jesus through His love. Why not? It worked in the Garden of Eden on the first Adam, so why not try it here in the wilderness? Satan's goal, as displayed in Matthew 4:1–11 was to seduce and tempt Jesus into choosing to follow Satan's instructions. Any attempt to ensnare Jesus by using a follower of His would risk Jesus seeing through Satan's plan, resulting in angering Jesus for using one of His beloved as bait.

Jesus' whole reason for being on earth in this human state was out of His and His Father's agape unconditional love for humans. If Satan decided to put one of the precious beloved people in Jesus' visual scope, he ran the risk of engaging, by mere visual contact, the implicit reminder of that agape love for mankind. Not that Jesus necessarily forgot about that love, but this is potentially a reason God sent Jesus into the wilderness and away from people for the temptation to have any effect. It was a quite clever decision by Satan not to risk using people this time, with *this* Adam. Never mind the fact that there was no one else in the wilderness to use, an interesting deviation from the setting of the temptation in the Garden of Eden!

The scene of the Garden of Eden was beautiful and perfect, full of the blessing of the Lord, and God's son Adam was in full control. Enter one temptation of Satan through Eve, and Adam stumbled and fell. Flash forward a few thousand years. The wilderness scene was dark and evil and was Satan's domain. Enter Satan's temptations … This picture of Jesus confronting the Devil from within his own realm and among his own wickedness foreshadows another similar circumstance that occurred immediately following Calvary. The glorious results parallel as well with Jesus submitting to God's will and emerging triumphant. (Hallelujah!)

Satan, now fully aware of the identity of the Messiah, after so many generations of searching, was surely clued in to the golden opportunity he was afforded by this apparent oversight in God's plan. Clearly the Devil's worldly pattern of thinking could not conceive of how this wasn't an accident by God. In fact, how would most people of the world today view the commission God made for His Son without the benefit of knowing the outcome? Whatever purpose God had, He was giving His archenemy, Satan, free shots at His beloved Son, and it was after having Him fast for forty days. This supposedly loving Father drew a bull's-eye on Jesus' back and separated Him from His brothers and everyone else, rendering Him alone in the middle of Satan's evil wilderness territory! The worldly legal view of that only begins at gross neglect and includes grave abuse, with some cruel and unusual punishment thrown in.

However this encounter was going to eventually manifest, Satan most certainly had been anticipating the moment since the garden. Satan did try many times to preempt this face-to-face encounter by enacting his slash-and-burn tactical brainchild—to kill all newborn, infant, and toddler male children that might possibly rise up and destroy his kingdom. He orchestrated this through King Herod, just after the Messiah's birth. Fearing the prophecies that called Jesus the coming king of the Jews, Herod, the current king over Judea during the time of Jesus' birth, had heard the rumor of the birth of the prophesied child king of the Jews. He ordered the slaughter of all the male children in Bethlehem under two years old in attempt to slay He who in Herod's mind threatened his life as king.

Of course Satan missed that opportunity because God forewarned Joseph in a dream to sidestep Herod and skip town with Mary and their son, baby Jesus. The slaughter ensued, but Jesus escaped unharmed. So the prophecy by the prophet Jeremiah was fulfilled that there was a voice in Rama to be heard of lamentation and weeping and great mourning, Rachel weeping for her children (Matthew 2:17–18 KJV). Several other times Satan had tried to kill the Messiah by attacking through the bloodline. However, even after launching those unsuccessful attacks, Satan remained the same devious, conniving manipulator he grew to become upon going rogue from being God's General Lucifer. You can be sure that Satan did not place all his eggs of trying to defeat God in the one basket of attempting to prematurely kill off the royal bloodline. The Devil remained steadfast in his preparation and planning for this prophesied encounter. From this wilderness decree of God concerning the tempting trials of Jesus, Satan gleaned opportunities and planned to make it the game-ending showdown.

Satan knew all too well that if he could succeed in tempting Jesus away from His Messianic purpose and calling, then he would effectively recreate his successful fall scene from the Garden of Eden. The Devil set about ordering his chief demonic commanders to display, for Satan to choose from all of the most seductive, most historically successful, and most deadly weapons and fiery darts forged in the deepest, hottest pits of hell itself. Satan was going to try to end the war and defeat God right then and there, once and for all. So what were the ultimate, premium crafted, premier weapons that Satan choose for his most seductively beautiful, murderous plot? Which device had the greatest potential of cracking that blessed spiritual armor Jesus wore around all the time? What were the most opportune perceived weaknesses in Jesus the human, which promised the greatest temptation of the Holy One of God?

Satan the Accuser

Having myself completed a forty-day and night fast where I consume no food and I drink only water and 100 percent fruit and vegetable juices for 40 days, I can tell you that by week two of my last fast, I was ready to call it quits. I wouldn't really quit, but the point is, I was so very hungry, particularly after perhaps the hardest part, days two and three, the Devil's temptations and those of my flesh were relentless. For me, it was exactly as foretold. The enticing, seductive form of a beautiful angel of light spoke to me in a quiet version of a voice I believe was satanically auto-tuned and remixed to sound ultra-melodic and angelic. The voice said to me softly but very clearly as I was kneeling and praying, "It's okay now. You have done great! God really loves you for doing this fast, so you can stop now. God knows your heart, that it is in the right place, and He will fully honor your fast. It's okay to stop; you don't have to go on with it."

The message was crooned in such a sweet and encouraging manner, and after two days of fasting, when many people are most tempted, I couldn't help but consider it. I truly believe that indeed God would have honored my efforts if I had in fact done my very best but broke the fast for a meal or for a day or even if I ended the fast altogether, as the tempting voice had suggested. But take it to the bank that Satan would have been hounding me incessantly, trying to get me to feel condemned as a failure, even though it was he who tried to convince me to end the fast in the first place. That Devil will switch from instigator to accuser faster than a two-faced politician who is lying about his lies.

In fact, the Devil still tries to condemn me about the spicy cayenne pepper and spice I added to liven up the 100 percent pure vegetable juice I drank for dinner. I just tell him to shut up and go sit down somewhere because he is a spoiled, defeated foe and has no effect on me. It's pretty cool that he actually obeys like a trained dog when you get the hang of commanding him with the authority of God's Word in your voice. However, as Jesus said, rejoice not at the obedience of the spirits to your command; rather rejoice that our names are written in heaven (Luke 10:20)!

I believe Satan, that old serpent, probably laid that same load of hooey on Adam and Eve after they fell in the Garden of Eden. Satan is called the Accuser, and he will always be that ... the same yesterday, today and until his never-ending date of torment with the beast and the false prophet in the lake of fire and brimstone (Revelation 20:10). Can't you just see God standing at the gate of the Garden of Eden pointing and directing all three disobeyers,

Adam, Eve, and the Serpent, out of and away from the garden? Out of His holy, righteous, legal compliance and obligation, the Father of creation had to do it, in spite of - even because of His perfect Love, God's forever-optimistic heart now heavy from compassionate, parental disappointment.

I've envisioned the picture of the Serpent, Adam, and Eve sauntering out of the garden, Adam and Eve sulking, the Dragon-Serpent frustrated, struggling to get used to now having to move about by slithering around on his belly (Genesis 3:14). But in between fits of coughing up dirtballs, I'm all but sure the Serpent was hysterically laughing his "sssinister" laugh, trying to belittle and shame Adam about Adam's sorry attempt at sewing those fig leaves together as aprons for clothes. Admittedly, that remedial fiasco probably even made God Almighty chuckle and shake His holy head as He gave to Adam and Eve coats of skins to wear. Knowing his accusatory character, I believe Satan was probably trying to grease Adam's goose about that one throughout the better part of the nine hundred years he lived after the banishment.

Jesus Vulnerable and Tempted?

With Jesus soon finishing up His forty-day fast, which likely didn't include any food or any juice, and may not have included water either or very little, the Lord was sustained through faith exclusively by the glory of God the Father. Jesus, remaining in constant prayer with praise and worship, was perhaps only sustained by the rivers of living water flowing within the Lord. Of course Jesus was still operating without taking up His divinity scepter. At this point, He was still as much a human being as you and me. Jesus was most assuredly physically famished and dehydrated as the forty-day fast rendered His body physically vulnerable to temptation, especially by the prospect of consuming real food.

If the account is read too quickly, one might say food is exactly what the Devil tempted Jesus with for the first temptation. It certainly sounds quite logical at this stage in Jesus' fast. However, through prayerful meditation on God's Word in Matthew 4:3 KJV, the Holy Spirit reveals that it really wasn't a food temptation at all. The bread was merely a decoy. The Devil likely surmised that Jesus was far too spiritually connected and engaged with His Papa upstairs, what with all the spiritual "text messages" and personal "tweets" and "Skype" calls of prayer the Lord continuously engaged in with the Father, to fall for the old hunger games trick. If Satan's temptation was only about getting Jesus to eat, then instead of suggesting that Jesus turn the stones to bread, you can believe Satan could himself have produced bread or for that matter instantly produced an entire full-blown, decked-out, mile-long feast of the royal order. Satan clearly was aware that this simply was not an area of weakness or a particularly temptable virtue of Jesus.

It was no accident that in the first temptation of The Christ following His physical and spiritual impartation of the Holy Ghost, and during the height of the Savior's first physical suffering, the area of the Savior in which Satan chose to attack was the mind—specifically the cognitive area of Jesus' Sonship perception. When the Tempter came to Jesus, his very first word was "*if*". That word *if*, which Satan deployed as his first point of attack, the poisoned tip of the first arrow, his first fiery dart, was at the same time deceivingly rudimentary and treacherously clever. This dichotomy would prove to be a hallmark of Satan and his devices. The goading word "If", used in the scriptural context of Satan's first deceptive wilderness snare for Jesus, was not phrased as the classic query, "If X then Y." That scenario carries the indefinite question, "If X is indeed X, then Y should necessarily be Y." The more likely meaning of Satan's *if* in this context refers to the more affirmative "since" definition as in, "Since X is in fact the case, then Y should necessarily follow." With a touch of charm, "since" becomes an affirmative, feather-stroking seduction, sentimentally invoking the proverbial arm around the shoulder cue from some nefarious how to win friends and seduce people manual.

Consider Satan's "if" in this context, if you will. The classic schoolyard scene where a new kid, innocent if naive, who is eager to make friends, is approached by a seemingly popular lad. The lad waltzes up to the new kid bearing the Cheshire grin of a cat that swallowed the canary, quipping, "Hey! So, I heard you can swing a mean bat … if you are good, let's see it." He shoves a ball and baseball bat into the newbie's hand. Then the little twerp puts his arm around newbie's shoulder and says, "Now give it a good shot, 'cause everyone's watching." Meanwhile, with his arm around newbie's shoulder, he gently rotates newbie's body just so and then pats him on the back before backing up to where his friends are standing.

Those friends are already chuckling at the real prospect of witnessing their devious plan unfold before their eyes. As the eager-to-please new kid grips the bat, knowing he's played baseball for years and this should be a cinch of an icebreaker, likely leading to instant friends and fame, he tosses the ball up and takes his best swing. To his anticipated delight, he connects flush with the ball, sending it hurtling through the playground atmosphere, realizing only too late that the ball happens to be speeding mercilessly straight for the principal's big office window. Operation humiliate, successful.

Matthew 4:3 says, "And when the tempter came to Him, he said, 'If thou be the Son of God, command that these stones be made bread.'" This proposal of Satan wasn't about the bread at all, even though the Bible says Jesus was in fact very hungry (Matthew 4:2 KJV). Satan was all too familiar with God's operational methods, processes and policies, as the transgressing of them is what got him tossed from heaven. The Devil was fully aware that Jesus would not have been able to turn those stones to bread *in His human state* without the direct command of God the Father. This knowledge accounts for the way Satan phrased the question, and I paraphrase, "If and since You are the Son of God, the actual second person of the Trinity, and thereby God Himself, surely with Your great abilities You can end this starvation of Yours right here and now. You know, it can't even be good for Your health as a human ... the body needs its food. So just give Your body the nourishment it craves, turn this stone into bread, and end Your suffering." Satan's devious plan of misdirection might likely have been rooted in an attempt to get Jesus to be homesick, in a sense, for heaven and for His divinity role.

Satan needed to convince Jesus to access pride in His divinity role. Once the Devil encouraged Jesus, who had willingly (at the ordinance of the Father) set aside His divinity scepter to be born of woman and become 100 percent fully human, to miss being in God fully as at the beginning (John 17:5 KJV), and once Satan compelled of Jesus a greater longing to return to that divine oneness role with the Father, then that would have been the Devil's foothold. Immediately, Satan would have begun trying to amplify that longing to the point where Jesus might be willing to consider tapping into His divinity to regain the power of that role, thereby foregoing the will of the Father. Once again, the Devil failed to comprehend the absolute humility of our Messiah.

Truly, this first temptation had nothing to do with food; it was on a much more personal level. Satan knew from that prophetic edict God gave at expulsion from the garden that the seed of Eve would bruise his head. Therefore, once Jesus had accessed His divinity to perform a divine act outside the Father's will, even for just a moment, He would consequently no longer be fully human. It would have immediately disqualified Jesus from being the redeeming substitute for the sins of mankind. Jesus was able to be our human substitute and full redeemer from the penalty of our sin precisely because He walked the earth as a fully human man in perfect obedience to the Father, conquering sin, while never once picking up His divinity scepter throughout His entire earthly life and ministry. The Savior was obedient to God's divine wisdom and perfect plan throughout His human plight, despite Jesus' carnal and human reservations as revealed through His temptations, and explicitly at the garden of Gethsemane. Jesus remained faithful even unto death.

What Satan did not and could not understand, and what he underestimated in Jesus, is the power of God's agape love for the Lord, and indeed for the humans God created. The bible says the devil is a liar and the truth is not in him (John 8:44 KJV). The truth of this mystery will elude Satan, but unfortunately many people today miss this revelation because they are misled by lukewarm Churches that are suffering the crisis of lack of faith. For fear of potentially losing sensitive attendees, these church leaders preach only passive 'faith-safe' messages based solely on worldly logic and carnal experience. While those sermons are easily digestible messages, they do not require faith in the power of God's word. These soft and pacifying sermons do not stretch and build up the faith of the people at all, and this causes people to miss the revelation of the divine synergy that God wants, and has always wanted with His people. It begins with having faith in God's word and preaching in that confidence. Then people are awakened by the blessed revelation of the Holy Spirit through proper faith and truth preaching and teaching.

As the revealed truth causes spiritual scales to fall from the eyes of people, Christians begin to recognize who they really are, who God created them to be as His very children. God's plan and desire for man was clearly established in Genesis 1:27-30. "And God blessed (Adam and Eve [mankind]) and said "be fruitful and multiply and replenish the earth and subdue it: and have dominion over the fish of the sea, and over the fowl of the air and over every living thing that moveth upon the earth." God also gave man the job of "dressing" and "keeping" the garden in Genesis 2:15. Did God intend for this to be how mankind operated only during the time of Adam and Eve in the Garden of Eden or did God make those decrees because that is exactly what He wanted for His creation? God says in Malachi 3:6 "I am the LORD and I change not...", so God's original desire for man is still His desire for man today.

When people grow in faith through hearing the revelation of God's word (Romans 10:17 KJV), the Holy Spirit reveals to them how to receive and operate in the critical faith and obedience synergy with God the Father. They can then enter into the extremely powerful truths of the manifested Word of God. Throughout His earthly ministry, Jesus repeated the concept numerous times that even He can do nothing of himself but what He sees His Father do, that is what He does, and what He hears His Father say, that is what He says (John 5:19-20, 30-34, John 14:6-7, 10 KJV). In other words, the only reason Jesus was so perfectly effective, is because Jesus didn't act or speak unless it was directly ordered from our heavenly Father (through the Holy Spirit). When Jesus saw God act, He copied the Father. When He would hear the voice of the Father by the Holy Spirit, Jesus would verbally 'copy and paste' the Father's words. Jesus was batting 1000 with each miracle attempt because operating strictly in obedience to the Father brings unparalleled faith. Of course God wants to heal people in His perfect timing and love, and Jesus was obeying God doing exactly what the Creator of the universe told Him to do. The message translation of the bible in Matthew 11: 29 MSG refers to this synergy as the unforced rhythms of grace.

The tool that God has given us today to spiritually access the walking-with-God synergy that Jesus had and Adam had in the garden before the fall, without being swayed by today's sin and worldly lusts, is the tool of fasting and praying. As evidenced by the Lord's walk with God the Father and His earthly ministry, Jesus demonstrated that a regular fasting and prayer lifestyle was the essential component to maintaining that heightened state of spiritual connectivity and relationship with the Father. This is such a vital part of the life of today's Christian who seeks effective kingdom of God living. When people grow in faith through hearing the revelation of God's word (Romans 10:17 KJV), and the Holy Spirit reveals to them how to receive and operate in the critical faith and obedience synergy with God the Father, they can then enter into the extremely powerful truths of the manifested Word of God and begin to really do the works that Jesus did and greater works (John 14:12 KJV).

Maintaining that divine flow of connectivity with Yahweh (YHWH), Jesus demonstrated for us how to operate in the truth of dominion as a human, first over self and then over the environment. It is in this connected state that Jesus realized and reveals with the help of the Holy Ghost (John 14:16–20 KJV), that even in human form He could still maintain exceedingly great intimacy and synergy with the Father. Granted it was not exactly like in the beginning, at the foundation of the world, but the parallels of the beginning, and of Jesus' ministry reveal how similar it really is. (This parallel of Jesus' terre-foundational and humane oneness with the Father will be explored a little later.) This allowed Jesus to more clearly see and hear the Father to mimic His heavenly actions and words in the earth. The gospels don't specifically reveal exactly when Jesus learned this particular lesson, but fasting and prayer clearly were very integral and vital parts of His life, daily walk, and ministry, as well as the lives and walks and ministries of His disciples.

Kingdom Nourishment for Spiritual Development

FIFTH COURSE
THE LIES OF BABYLON

> Lest Satan should get an advantage of us: for we are not ignorant of his devices (2 Corinthians 2:11 KJV).

The temptations and snares Satan has set up in this world are designed specifically to keep the masses ensnared and enslaved to his Babylonian system of toil as people try to meet their own needs without God. However, Satan has diabolically set up the world system in such a clever way that it encourages toil (struggle to live in one's own strength without using God's strength which works through faith), by occasionally rewarding token toilers with charmed worldly riches. The Devil has even deceivingly called it "the good life" or "the American dream" and has made it very seductive for people to continue toiling and sweating, hoping they too might one day be similarly lucky.

If someone happens to either through luck or through "hard work" reach a pinnacle of worldly economic status, especially after passing through or altogether bypassing two or three economic tiers along the way, immediately the Devil's Babylonian snares of pride and self-exaltation begin to materialize. History details quite clearly that should one happen to be born into a wealthy, high-society family, there is truly a special brand of entitlement and self-deification snare that Satan has reserved for that individual. Whether or not they succumb to the Enemy's snare is another matter concerning God's grace and the individual's heart, faith and up-bringing (Ephesians 2:8, Proverbs 4:23, Proverbs 22:6 KJV). The Babylonian idols of wealth and status, and even political party and race bickering which the Devil has slyly set up in this world system can be very effective snares, making it not only exceedingly difficult to escape but also sensibly undesirable to refute, not to mention unpopular (Matthew 24:4–15, 19:21–26; Luke 18:22–27; Revelation 12:9, 20:3 KJV).

In the first of the wilderness temptation of Christ, Satan was attempting to stoke and stir up pride in the divinity Jesus willingly laid aside to fulfill the will and ordinance of God the Father. Satan was attempting to bait Jesus into doing his own bidding, goading the Lord into alleviating the hunger pangs He was suffering by turning the stone into bread. While faith by itself is indeed quite strong, it is not dynamic enough in and of itself to generate the power to produce miracles. Neither worldly logic nor faith in one's self ever produced any miracles, not even for Jesus. There was always something additional, another ingredient present that provided the power to activate the miracles.

The faith of Jesus Christ was not built upon His own ability to perform miracles. This was the blessed meekness and humility of the Savior (Matthew 10:24, 11:27; John 5:17-19, 5:30–31 KJV). If Jesus had attempted to do any miracles outside of the will of the Father, and without the dunamis power of God's Word backing what God told Jesus to do, it would have been an epic failure. Jesus would have sunk like a rock right there in the Sea of Galilee, and both He and Peter would have been treading water if Jesus had stayed out there on the water a second after God told Him to get into the boat (John 14:10 KJV). Therein lies the force behind the temptation of what Satan's baiting statement inferred, "If you are the Son of God ..." Satan's bait carried more of a prodding ellipsis sentiment rather than the inferred question mark.

What was it that tempted Jesus, the Anointed One? What could have caused the Messiah Savior, begotten Son of God to pause and consider? It was Jesus' role as our intercessor and Savior that required Him to lay aside His own divinity. Satan was trying his best to form a wedge in the midst of this intrinsic dichotomy of Jesus' identity as deity, as second person of the Trinity, as God, and Jesus' role as Savior, Intercessor, and obedient Son. Satan was trying to get the always-obedient Jesus to (paraphrasing intent for dramatic effect) "Shoulder up a little. You are God! God shouldn't be suffering hunger pangs. You can just make this rock into bread Yourself. Why wait for dear old Dad to give you His word? You are a grownup now. Just do it Yourself. You can save God the trouble. After all, He gave You the ability; You were born with it. It's Your birthright!"

Can't you just picture the Tempter arrogantly laying that same load of crap on all the angels in heaven before his fall, repeating that same junk over and over, angel after angel like a door-to-door salesman? Lucifer eventually convinced enough angels to join his army of one third of heavenly hosts in his bid to overthrow God (Revelation 12:3-4 KJV). That load of hooey worked on the lot of them, so why shouldn't Satan at least try it here on the Son of man, especially now that Jesus was clearly under some pressure during this wilderness test. He had not eaten in forty days, and He was most certainly malnourished and hungry. The nutritional breakdown of Jesus' body had to have some adverse effects. One would think Jesus' body would have been warring against itself and against Jesus' mind, even taking the Devil's side of things, saying, "Yeah, come on, Jesus, eat already, dude!" (Sound familiar? John 4:31–34 KJV.) "You haven't had any food in forever it feels like …" Jesus' flesh was likely pleading. "Can't You just turn that stone into a piece of toast or an English muffin!"

Nonetheless, through all the pressure, Jesus' spirit remained in supreme command of His mind and body. How did He do it? He showed us how and told us in Matthew 11:27–30 KJV to watch Him as He demonstrated how He did it, how He maintained that special Father Son relationship with Jehovah Elohim, Abba Father God in heaven, and then just copy Him. After all, that's how it worked within the relationship of Jesus and God the Father. But that did not stop Satan from trying to squeeze his fiery darts past Jesus' shield of faith. "Surely if you are indeed the Holy Anointed One, Son of the Most High God, then why should You suffer like this? You shouldn't be starving and such … Since You are the real deal, the Second Person of the Trinity and God Himself, it should be simple enough for you to end this. Why God would want anyone suffering anyway, especially for Himself? So just command these stones to be bread and end Your suffering. It would prove Your power as Son of God and at the same time end those hunger pangs You've been feeling for months."

In the wilderness, the backyard of the Prince of the Power of the Air, Jesus was physically blinded to any real evidence of His Sonship and thereby tempted to doubt. The Savior overcame the temptation by blocking that fiery dart disguised as a merciful suggestion to end His suffering with His shield of faith. Jesus perceived the truth behind the suggestion and held fast to faith in His Sonship through the onslaught of temptation, despite not seeing evidence or feeling particularly loved and protected and physically nourished as a beloved Son.

This very same temptation would resurface later as Jesus prophesied in Luke 4:23 KJV, saying "Ye will surely say unto me this proverb, Physician, heal thyself ..." which came to pass in Luke 23:35, 37 KJV. "And the people stood beholding. And the rulers also with them derided him, saying, 'He saved others; let him save himself, if he be the Christ, the chosen one of God ... And saying, if thou be the king of the Jews, save thyself." Notice that the forthcoming temptation was prophetically revealed to Jesus. This is another instance where the close walk with the Father and relationship with the Holy Spirit yields foreknowledge of what will happen. Jesus didn't only know things in advance because He was the only begotten Son of God. The Apostle Paul reveals in Romans 12:6

KJV "Having then gifts differing according to the grace that is given to us, whether prophecy, let us prophecy according to the proportion of faith". According to the proportion of faith means it is not only given to certain people, but rather those with the proportion of faith have access. And we know that faith comes by hearing, and hearing by the word of God (Romans 10:17 KJV). Jesus said that the Holy Spirit of Truth will reveal to us the things to come, just as He revealed things to come to Jesus (John 16:13-15 KJV). Our beloved, righteous, and faithful Savior remained steadfast, giving praise unto the Father, throughout the torturous gauntlet of His destiny even to the end.

As the maturing sons and daughters of God aspire to continue growing in grace by faith, and as we receive greater measures of grace, building up our most holy faith through praying in the spirit, we practice greater faith in the face our own temptation wilderness. We even overcome our own versions of the garden of Gethsemane as doubt gets swallowed up in victory. It brings to mind with the fondness of brotherly love of all the many martyrs gone before throughout the ages and those of today who are currently under duress, for whom we cease not in prayer and faithful thanksgiving for their imminent victories.

Jesus' Walk

Jesus' shield of faith answer to Satan's first temptation was to quote the very Scripture that embodied the faith and embodied the walk of Jesus' life and ministry. Matthew 4:4 KJV says, "But He answered and said, 'It is written, Man shall not live by bread alone, but by every word that proceedeth out of the mouth of God.'" Because of Jesus' walk with the Father, which included a continuous fasting and praying lifestyle, Jesus secured a lockstep synergy with God the Father's will (Matthew 11:27 KJV). This synergistic walk with God and the divine benefits that resulted pervade the Scriptures, from pre-fall Adam (Genesis 1:31, 2:15, 19–20, and 23 KJV), to Noah (Genesis 6:9, 22 KJV), and to Abraham (Genesis 12:1, 4, 14:22, 15:6, 18:17–19 KJV), Isaac (Genesis 26:1–5, particularly verses 6, 12–13 KJV), Jacob (Genesis 28:7, 10–19, 20–22 KJV), and Joseph (Genesis 39:2, 41:38–42 KJV) and continues even through Moses (Exodus 3:10, 4:31, 5:1 KJV). The precept prevails in the life of Joshua (Joshua 1:5–11 KJV).The walk of synergy with the will of God is the consistent theme through the Scriptures as recorded in the lives of David from youth through his ascension and reign as king, with Daniel and his friends, Shadrach, Meshach, and Abed-nego, and King Solomon, at least up until the tail end of his reign when the Devil, through lust, finally got the best of him.

The prophet Isaiah revealed a significant and profound prophecy of the Matthew 11:27–30 KJV revelation of Jesus' walk in Isaiah 55:1–5 KJV. God is revealing to us through these verses, as He does in starkly repetitive, simplistic patience throughout the Scriptures, that we receive His blessing when we walk by faith, as we hearken diligently to the voice of God, observing to do or obeying God's Word. God relays His word to us through the Bible and by His sent word, which is most frequently delivered by way of the still, small voice of the Holy Spirit. God's voice is also sent through His messenger angels or delivered through a prophet or an anointed minister of the gospel, which includes but is not limited to some preachers.

The believer does not have to be a priest or a 30 year bible scholar to receive a word from God. A lifetime of unparalleled theological academia does not more greatly prepare one to receive a word from the Lord than simply being born again, truly loving God, and making oneself available in communion with Him. By that same token, not all "professional" preachers are anointed of God. (See John 15:2, 8:33–47, 6:47–64; Matthew 7:13–23 KJV). As the truly faithful listen for the voice of God, hear the voice of God with ears of hearing, and obey the voice of God, they will experience Jesus' abundant life of John 10:10 KJV. The whole tenth chapter of John tells the story quite exquisitely.

The Second Temptation of Christ

With temptation plan A thwarted by Jesus' shield of faith, which was deftly followed up by the quick and mighty sword of the word, Satan prepared to launch his second attack, his backup plan to ensnare Jesus in the wilderness. This time the Devil decided to get Jesus to a different location and proceeded to attack Jesus' mind once again. Now Satan attacked by tempting a different basic human reflex, typically engaged to ensure self-preservation. This seduction, not unlike the first, was a subtle misdirection and was once again aimed at the sonship perception of Jesus. Matthew 4:5–6 KJV says, "Then the Devil taketh him up into the holy city, and setteth him on a pinnacle of the temple, and saith to him, 'If thou be the Son of God, cast thyself down; for it is written, He shall give his angels charge concerning thee; and in their hands they shall bear thee up, lest at any time thou dash thy foot against a stone.'" I believe Jesus was probably stuck in the midst of some of His greatest temptation at that very instant. I believe The Lord was also caught right in between wanting to laugh hysterically, and wanting to slap the taste out of the Devil's mouth after the very first syllable! But let's back up and consider first things first.

The Tempter takes Jesus up into Jerusalem and sets Him on the pointy tip of the top of one of the steeples of the temple. Then the Devil, in unmitigated audacity, huffs at the Lord, as He is balancing on a tiny pinnacle of the synagogue, and again I paraphrase, "Since You are the Son of God, You certainly shouldn't be afraid up here. All You have to do is cast Yourself down (at *my* request) …" Satan repeats his sinister jab at Jesus' perception of His sonship. Notice in Jesus' response to the first temptation, while Jesus effectively rebutted the surface temptation of the issue of bread and even did it by quoting Scripture, He did not exactly address to His attacker with pointed clarity His perception of His place in God's family tree, which is what Satan actually attacked. This is why in the second temptation of Jesus in Mark 4:5–6, Satan systematically attacked in the same area as in the first attempt. When one looks at Satan's systematic approach in tempting the Savior, as told in Matthew's account of the wilderness temptations of Christ, Satan's first two approaches were different than the last, and Jesus' responses also changed.

The perceptive state of mind is what the evil one's database of a millennium's worth of field work case study in human psychology revealed as his most pliable and impressionable inroad to dissect and dislodge the faith of Jesus. This data betrayed the most historically successfully harnessable human impulse whereby Satan could force compliance in the doing of his evil bidding. Consequently, without a direct, unyielding assertion conveying fastidious devotion to His Sonship, even while in the midst of all sensory torment, Jesus was fated to endure yet another similar attack. However, the Lord would be quick to learn His lesson.

Context

Now before we proceed, let's go to three places in the gospels for an important contextual reference. The first place is the only other gospel that gives a detailed account of the post-baptismal temptation of Jesus in the wilderness. In the gospel of Luke, who was the physician disciple of Christ, the record of Jesus' wilderness temptation, as detailed in Luke 4:1–13 KJV, is virtually identical to Matthew's account in terms of the specifics of the dictation. In fact, the two accounts basically differ in only one detail. In Dr. Luke's version, the order of Satan's second and third temptations was flipped from the order in Matthew's version. In the gospel of Luke, the second time Satan came to Jesus to tempt Him into doing his bidding outside the will of God the Father, the Devil offered Jesus the power and glory of all the kingdoms of the world (earth) (Luke 4:5–7 KJV).

Jesus' response to Satan's first temptation as recorded by Dr. Luke was the same as that recorded by Matthew, a direct Bible quotation concerning the bread temptation, without addressing Satan's attack on the Jesus' perception of His sonship (Luke 4:4 KJV). Jesus' response to the second temptation according to Dr. Luke's account revealed similar maturation, as did Matthew's account of the second temptation, even though the second and third temptations were flipped in the two gospels. In both gospels Jesus' second reply quoted the appropriate Scripture, as in His first response. However, at the second temptation, both gospel accounts record Jesus' reply carrying a much more focused and authoritative tone.

Dr. Luke's gospel reveals that Jesus replied to the temptation of Satan offering lordship over all the kingdoms of Earth by commanding, "Get thee behind me, Satan: for it is written thou shalt worship the Lord your God, and him only shalt thou serve" (Luke 4:8 KJV). In the second temptation of Christ in the wilderness, Jesus stepped up the authoritative tone and the specificity in His scriptural response, indicating Jesus' developed awareness of what was required to effectively address the core of Satan's temptation. This is very key for us to realize. As we progress through our lives facing various temptations, which will continue as long as we are in the flesh, we too, like Jesus, are to mature in defensive/offensive combat skill with the help of the Holy Spirit. We must get better and better at more effectively "backing down the Tempter" with our shield of faith *and responding* with the sword of the Word when Satan attacks. We must also grow in God's grace and wisdom to maintain a spirit-led kingdom walk when our selfish flesh yearns for carnality.

In revealed kingdom of God truth, the Devil and his seed, sin; the autonomous power of the kingdom of darkness are defeated

(Genesis 3:15, John 16:7-11 KJV). Jesus fully accomplished that after Golgotha where the Lord willingly received the physical death consequence for the sins of mankind, and His Spirit descended into Hell to receive makind's sin penalty of God's wrath (Isaiah 53:9-12 KJV), before ascending once again to the earth, to His disciples and ultimately to His Father (John 16:7-11, 33 KJV). This was Jesus's purpose, and He fully completed it (John 19:30 KJV). The only power the Devil has, now that Jesus has *finished* the task for which He was sent, is that which people give him through fear. Indeed Satan can manifest himself in those who give him power and personal access by extending their faith to him, instead of fearing only God (2 Corinthians 2:11, Ephesians 6:10-18 KJV). For the believer who is walking in the truth of God's Word by faith, not by sight, the light, the understanding of God's perfect love dispels and casts out fear (1 John 4:18 KJV) and the Devil is underfoot.

The way God by the Holy Spirit helps us to grow from grace to grace and from faith to faith is by allowing certain specific trials in our lives. When properly perceived, these trials become for the Christian opportunities to strengthen our faith, encouraging us to believe a little less in what we see with our fleshy eyes and, *in spite of what we see,* to trust a little more in the truth of God's eternal word. Hebrews 11:1 says "Now faith is the substance of things hoped for and the evidence of things not seen [or not yet revealed to the physical senses]". For those who trust only in what they see, how easily can their lives be controlled by manipulation? If David Blaine and David Copperfield can make you think you see something that isn't there, how much more can the Father of Lies and Deceiver of the whole world (Revelation 12:9 KJV) control those for whom seeing is believing? Without this key revelation igniting us, Christians today are fated to remain stagnant and immature in their faith walk. And a stagnant Christian is a manageable Christian in the eyes of Satan.

Now, let's examine the revelation of Satan's deceptive tactics. As we've seen, Satan is a liar and the father of lies. We know from the book of Genesis that Satan approached Eve in the form of a serpent. The Bible is not explicit as to whether Satan transformed himself into a serpent or demonically possessed the serpent to do his bidding. We also don't know unequivocally from Scripture if all the animals could talk or if this serpent was the only animal in the Garden of Eden that was talking. What we can glean, however, are clues from other areas of the Bible. I believe that as the verse in Genesis 3 says, the serpent was more cunning than all the other beasts, meaning none of the other animals were on the intellectual level (even of verbal speech) as the serpent.

A dragon or serpent would indeed resemble a snake-like animal that slithers about on its belly eating dust, when its arms, legs, wings, or whatever else it might have had were removed as per God's decree in Genesis 3:14 KJV. Why would God say you will go about slithering on your belly as a result of your transgression, if the serpent was already slithering about on it's belly? The serpent in the Garden of Eden must have been some sort of dragon-esque creature because the Devil is also referred to in Revelation 12:9 KJV as the Great Dragon. Yet even as a reptilian dragon, the Devil was able to reveal himself to Eve in a manner that did not startle or threaten her. Why? She had been taught by her husband Adam that humans were to have dominion over all the animals and beasts, so there was no fear in Adam and Eve of anything that moved on the earth because they were walking in dominion at this point. This clever Dragon Serpent proceeded to charm Eve into believing his cunning, deceptive words over what her husband should have told her, that which God had decreed concerning to eat or not to eat of the fruit of a particular tree.

Eve knew part of what God had decreed because she actually attempted to quote it to the Serpent. Except she got it incomplete…. or at least she did not quote the full truth in answering the serpents question. The serpent asked her if it wasn't true that God said they could eat of every tree in the garden. She responded by saying, "We may eat of the fruit of the trees of the garden: But of the fruit of the tree which is in the midst of the garden, God hath said ye shall not eat of it, neither shall ye touch it, lest ye die." That was a misrepresentation of what God said. God never said that Adam and Eve could not eat the fruit of the tree in the midst of the garden, and the serpent perceived that erroneous claim by Eve. The breakdown, however, was ultimately to Adam's charge, as it was his God-given responsibility to make sure Eve was fully clear about what the rules of the garden were. So Adam either misquoted God to Eve, or Adam did not duly express to Eve the proper importance of getting this edict of God right. So, Eve likely just forgot what Adam told her and then she botched it up when trying to remember under Satan's pressure.

There was in fact a tree that God placed in the midst of the garden, of which Adam and Eve were freely allowed to eat. Genesis 2:9 KJV reveals that there were two trees in the midst of the garden: the Tree of Life and the Tree of Knowledge of Good and Evil. Eve should have specified that God forbade the eating of the Tree of Knowledge of Good and Evil, rather than stating that they were not to eat of the tree in the midst of the garden. Notice that the Serpent recognized this error and took that as his cue, proceeding to guide Eve's reference back over to the Tree of Knowledge of Good and Evil. At this pivotal point, the serpent deceptively usurped Eve's position of leadership because he now had addressed an uncertainty in Eve. By seducing her with slick words and building her trust the serpent appeared in the form of a friend, however his motives and his entire sinister purposes were evil to the core. The Scriptures are full of accounts of these deceptive Trojan horse tactics, of which Satan here shows authorship.

One of the most revealing descriptions of Satan's deceptive tactics is described in the warning Jesus gave, saying in Matthew 7:15 KJV, "Beware of false prophets, which come to you in sheep's clothing, but inwardly are ravening wolves" (Mark 13:6; Luke 21:8 KJV). The apostle Paul warns the believers of the church at Corinth by explaining in his second letter to them in the eleventh chapter and verse 14, "And no marvel; for Satan himself is transformed into an angel of light." So we also must take the cue and keep from looking for a big scary monster when Satan does come because He will not let on his true identity. We must stay watchful, for he will be as cunning and crafty as possible in trying to ensnare us as he was with Eve. Satan will likely even pose as or involve an unwitting good friend of ours (like he did with Jesus using the Apostle Peter in Matthew 16:23 KJV). God will certainly reveal the truth to us, and if we are continuously fasting and praying and in lockstep with the will of God, just like Jesus was, we will live in a place that is spiritually sensitive enough to hear from the Holy Spirit of truth, all those things that are to come, and kingdom instructions from the Father even as Jesus heard them and followed them.

The third place of reference to help give us perspective is John 1:1–7, 10, and 14 KJV. While these verses are quite familiar, they bear review, particularly in the context of Jesus' second temptation accounts in both Matthew's and Luke's gospels. Interestingly, the Holy Spirit does not inspire John in his gospel to account for Jesus' temptations in the wilderness at all. And while the gospel of Mark refers to the post-baptismal temptation, Mark does not elaborate beyond the mere mention of the event.

What John is inspired to record, found in none of the other gospels or in the rest of the Bible with John's eloquence, is the nature of the personhood, identity and the very deity of the Word of God. John immediately establishes in Chapter 1:1 KJV "In the beginning was the Word, and the Word was with God, and the Word was God." In verses 2–7 he writes:

> The same was in the beginning with God. All things were made by him; and without him [the Word] was not anything made that was made. In him [the Word] was

life; and the life was the light of men. And the light [which is Holy Spirit revelation of the Truth, the person of the Word who is Jesus] shineth in darkness; and the darkness comprehended it not. There was a man sent from God whose name was John. The same came for a witness, to bear witness of the Light that all men through him [Jesus, the Light of Truth] might believe.

Verse 10 reads "He was in the world, and the world was made by him, and the world knew him not," and verse 14 says, "And the Word was made flesh and dwelt among us, (and we beheld his glory, as the glory of the only begotten of the Father,) full of grace and truth." John's Holy Ghost revelation of the personhood of the Word of God is starkly divine revelation. No human could ever conceive of this type of manifested truth. This truth is that the Word of God, which God spoke in the beginning at the foundation of the world, by which God created the heavens and the earth and formed everything therein, including man, was and is, in full revelation, a person.

John continues to shell shock those receiving his message, and one can only receive this message by the grace of God and by the spiritual quickening of the Holy Spirit (1 Corinthians 2:7–16; 2 Peter 1:2–4 KJV). Not only is the Word of God a person, but the person of the Word is the Spirit of Light in Truth, and the person and the Light existed from the beginning as one Spirit (Ephesians 6:17 KJV). That Spirit was God and Jesus Himself. So God spoke. What did God speak? The person and the Spirit of the Word, Jesus, who was in fact God (John 1:1 KJV)! And so what happened when God spoke God? A manifested explosion of God's will in the form of Light and Life sprang forth, cementing of all creation into its place. The darkness that was before the manifestation of the Word did not understand this truth of light, this person, Jesus.

Then John's gospel proceeds to reveal that the life of Jesus is that light that was pre-witnessed by the prophet John the Baptist, whom God sent to prepare the way. And John continues to illustrate the parallel of the darkness before creation not understanding the manifested light of God's Word, which produced this creation, with the darkness of the wilderness state of the world, including the Jewish people whom God chose, whom themselves also did not comprehend the truth and light of their very own Messiah. The world of the pre-Adamic blunder was originally created by the Word of God, manifested in the light of truth, and was perfect. Jesus, who was the Word manifested in truth of light, became flesh and dwelt among men in the darkness of the sinful world, and Jesus the sinless, spotless Lamb was also perfect. In both cases, it was the perfect light of the truth of the Word that was not comprehended by the darkness that was in the world.

The Hilarity; the Audacity

We glean greater understanding then of the full nature of the Word of God as a person, the very Spirit of God, a living spiritual weapon of light in the fight against darkness for the spirits and souls of men. This Word of God is a force that is "quick, and powerful, sharper than any two-edged sword, piercing even to the dividing asunder of soul and spirit, and of the joints and marrow, and is a discerner of the thoughts and intents of the heart" as Hebrews 4:12 tells us. Envision the hilarity that Jesus must have witnessed in Matthew's account of the second temptation as Satan fumbled through quoting Scriptures to Jesus, whose very essence is the light of truth and the Word, as John illuminated. I'm sure it was like watching a caveman fumble around with an actual Star Wars lightsaber (if you will) he had just found. The difference would be that although Satan knew firsthand the ultimate power of the word of God, having been booted out of heaven, forever banished and cast like lightning to the Earth for his treason, the fact that he even tried to access the power by quoting some seemingly relevant words in an attempt to get Jesus to acquiesce to the Devil's own request revealed his complete folly and ignorance in terms of how the power of the Word of God is accessed. So after fumbling around with the Word and not being able to access the power thereof, I picture the Neanderthal just throwing the "broken" lightsaber handle at Jesus in frustration.

Now as comical as that likely was, the dichotomy is that Jesus also had to have been veritably seething inside as He endured this particular test in the wilderness. As if the audacity already displayed by Satan wasn't enough in questioning Jesus' self-perception of His Sonship, the Devil proceeded to quote the Bible to Jesus. Satan, who spews only vomit and venom out of His corrupted, black, soulless pit, presumes to try to quote the word of God, to the *Word* Himself, Jesus! These sacred Scriptures are God's holy, inspired love notes to His beloved creation, and this foul impostor dared to inhale God's oxygen, and then fixed his filthy, vile mouth to form God's precious words with perverse intentions of hate, theft, murder and destruction (John 10:10 KJV). You can believe that it took every ounce of strength for Jesus not to grab His divinity scepter and clap His hands, sending Satan in to eternal oblivion at the very first syllable in defense of His Father's holy Word and the beloved sheep He was ordained to shepherd. The Bible says Jesus was tempted in pursuing the will of the Father. This, I believe, was the real temptation of the Lord.

The Trickster Uncovered; the Gift of Discernment

The word of God is the law of the universe, so why Satan thought he could tempt the Word who was the law of the universe, even though He was in human form, heaven only knows. But once again, the word says Jesus was in fact tempted. Jesus' 'shield-of-faith' answer to Satan's first temptation was to quote the very scripture that embodied the faith walk of Jesus' life and ministry. Matthew 4:4 KJV says "But He answered and said, 'It is written that man shall not live by bread alone, but by every word that proceedeth out of the mouth of God.'" Jesus' walk remained close with the Father through fasting and prayer with a lockstep Spirit led life to keep connected through faith in spite of the earthly and carnal realities which constantly war against the faith. This walk was prophesied throughout the Old Testament in the lives of many mighty men of God as related by Moses in the first books of the bible. Moses revealed that Adam in the Garden of Eden (pre-fall) possessed the walk in Genesis 1:31, Genesis 2:15, 19-20, 23 KJV. This walk was present with Noah as seen in Genesis 6:9, 22 KJV, with Abraham in Genesis 12:1, 4, Genesis 14:22, Genesis 15:6, Genesis 18:17-19 KJV. Also Isaac displayed the walk in Genesis 26:1-5, 6, and 12-13 KJV. Jacob also revealed the walk according to Moses in Genesis 28:7, 10-19, 20-22 KJV, as did Joseph in Genesis 39:2 KJV, and Genesis 41:38-42 KJV. Moses himself displayed the walk throughout his life as revealed in Exodus 3:10 – Exodus 4:25, 28-31 KJV, Exodus 5:1 KJV. Even Joshua also displayed such a close walk with God the father in Joshua 1, 5-11 KJV, as have other throughout the Old Testament including David, Shadrach, Meshach and Abednego, and in the life of King David and his son King Solomon. The prophet Isaiah also prophesied of the revelation of this walk which Jesus spoke of in Matthew 11:27-30 KJV, and it is found in Isaiah 55:1-5 KJV. In the New Testament, the Apostle John gives record of a convincing case of this walk relationship of Jesus and His followers, in the tenth chapter of his gospel. It is by this walk with God, with the Holy Spirit leading, and men ordering their Spirit to follow in lockstep with the Holy Spirit, that men develop spiritual discernment as the Holy Spirit of Truth reveals the things to come to those who are seeking it, seeking the kingdom of God, rather than seeking to satisfy the temporary carnal lust of the prideful, selfish flesh (Romans 8:1-21 KJV, and indeed the rest of Romans 8).

Jesus, in the second temptation account of Matthew, was balancing on the top of the synagogue's steeple, likely still light-headed from being rushed up there so quickly by Satan after already having low blood-sugar from the physical effects of the forty-day fast. Even so, do you believe Jesus would have been remotely tempted by Satan if he had approached the Lord as Hollywood portrays, in the form of having red, leathery skin, cloven hooves, two horns protruding from his forehead, a long pointy tail, and a pitchfork in his hand, saying, "Jump, Jesus, jump! The bible says the angels will catch you …" Of course not, right?

So how then would you say the Devil appeared to the Lord in a way that effectively tempted Him? Once again, 2 Corinthians 11:14–15 KJV says the Devil is transformed into an angel of light. Clearly there are a myriad of possibilities of how Satan could have approached Jesus and tempted Him, and the Bible is not explicit. The point is, how do you think Satan operates in the world today? Do you think all of his attacks and temptations are one dimensional and easy to recognize?

Believers must recognize we are not only under Satan's attack when it feels and looks like a demonic attack. A demon-possessed person does not always walk with his or her head spun backward, growling phrases in Latin with his or her spine bent over backwards in impossible formations. We must understand that the Devil and his demons do not always come to us looking evil and smelling like sulfur. Surely if that were the case, the trickster would not be able to perform what is revealed in Revelation 12:9 KJV as an effective deception of the whole world. If you are expecting the Devil to be so simple and obvious in his tactics, then Satan has you right where he wants you, completely fooled by his misdirecting Hollywood tricks.

So how did our Lord and Savior Jesus discern and perceive that this apparent angel of light who likely crooned with a sweet, melodic, angelic voice full of concern for Jesus' safety, quoting biblical promises of God's saving grace and His loving angels who would uphold Jesus? How did Jesus recognize that this impostor was in fact not the blessed merchant of light he likely appeared to be?

The Unforced Rhythms of Grace

One of the greatest blessings and spiritual gifts and abilities that developed as Jesus walked with God the Father is the same gift that developed as Noah and Moses walked with God the Father and that develops as any believer today walks with God the Father. Being in lockstep with the Father's will, as expressed in the lives of believers through God's grace and the gift of righteousness of our Lord Jesus Christ by way of the Holy Spirit (Romans 5:17 KJV), yields the spiritual gifts for reigning in life. Of these spiritual gifts, discernment is critical in order not to be deceived and led astray (1 Corinthians 2:9-16 KJV). The more time we spend in perpetual communion with our Lord Jesus Christ and our heavenly Father, basking in His agape divine love and recognizing, hearing and obeying His "still small voice" through the Holy Spirit, the more our spiritual eyes begin to open to God's kingdom truth. As we then continue to fellowship with God, we learn to live life leading with the spirit in agreement with the guidance of God's Holy Spirit. Carnal desires which arise in our flesh get shoved aside in favor of the riches of God's kingdom as our spirit comes alive and our spiritual eyes develop and stay open more often. Then God begins to lift the spiritual veil that was protecting our minds while we were still immature Christians and unable to bear the full, unbridled brightness of the higher spiritual light of truth in a healthy way (Acts 20:32).

With still further development through perpetual communion with God, by constant fasting and prayer and study of His written Word, our spiritual eyes, which become fully open, begin to focus and see more clearly. As we meditate on God's written Word and by His grace obey it and obey the sent word or the proceeded word from the mouth of God by way of the Holy Spirit, the muscles of our spiritual eyes, which control the ability to focus, begin to wax stronger and stronger. Ultimately we become able to clearly recognize in the spirit the things to which we were blind in the natural. This spiritual maturity is gained in one way and one way only (save for specific, instantaneous divine impartations or heavenly downloads/divine uploads, which are usually for a specific purpose and for an allocated duration of time, as in prophetic dreams and visions). Namely it is by growing in consistency and fervency in one's walk with God, including fasting, prayer, and meditation on the revealed truth of God's word in the bible. What follows is the development of the spiritual eyes, ears, and awareness, which all work together for the good of increasing spiritual discernment (Luke 10:19-24 KJV).

This spiritual discernment was mastered by our Master, the Lord Jesus, by the time of His temptations in the wilderness, and it gave Him the ability to perceive and discern the Devil's temptations. Even though Satan was himself a master magician, illusionist, and deceiver, being the Father of Lies (John 8:44 KJV), Jesus was able to easily and regularly throughout His earthly ministry discern all devils and demons, not because He was God but because of His developed spiritual maturity. As we've established, Jesus never touched His divinity scepter once during His whole earthly ministry, as that instantly would have invalidated Him as the stand-in and redeemer of humankind. By walking in Jesus' "easy sandals" of grace, truly repentant believers have been given the potential to achieve that same level of spiritual maturity so we too shall not be deceived by the deceptions of the Wicked One.

We simply must follow along in Jesus' footsteps, in the unforced rhythms of grace. We watch how He operated His ministry. We also take cues from the truths in the prophecies of old throughout the Old Testament and simply follow Jesus' example. This is a very vital demonstration by Jesus of how we are to access the same victorious, powerful lifestyle and spiritual walk He displayed. Jesus illuminated the concept in Matthew 11:27–30 KJV as a very intimate Father-Son relationship. He notes that this same Father-Son relationship, involving special divine knowledge and abilities, is not available anywhere else or in any other way but by such a close walk with the Father, and it cannot be attained by any means other than Jesus revealing it (Matthew 11:27, 13:9-11, Luke 10:22 KJV).

Those people to whom Jesus reveals Himself in the Light of Truth, those born again repentant believers who seek first the kingdom of God and His righteousness, can be partakers of the selfsame fellowship and walk with the Father, experiencing all of the same benefits. The Message translation is very eloquent in explaining this concept from Matthew 11:27–30 MSG. As Jesus is calling on believers to learn from Him how to return through faith to the state of sweatless dominion God always desired since creating Adam, and that Jesus restored to all believers in His finished work of the cross. Jesus was fully displaying this for us to learn and follow, but **only** those with faith that sees beyond what the carnal eyes see, and ears that hear beyond the voices of worldly reason can receive this truth.

> Jesus resumed talking to the people, but now tenderly. "The Father has given me all these things to do and say. This is a unique Father-Son operation, coming out of Father and Son intimacies and knowledge. No one knows the Son the way the Father does, nor the Father the way the Son does. But I'm not keeping it to myself; I'm ready to go over it line by line with anyone willing to listen. Are you tired? Worn out? Burned out on religion? Come to me. Get away with me and you'll recover your life. I'll show you how to take a real rest. Walk with me and work with me—watch how I do it. Learn the unforced rhythms of grace. I won't lay anything heavy or ill-fitting on you. Keep company with me and you'll learn to live freely and lightly."

God the Father gives freely to His sons and daughters all things pertaining to life and godliness (2 Peter 1:3 KJV). Believers must first exercise their free will and choose to repent from selfish carnality and follow Jesus in walking with God, eschewing the worldly, Babylonian idols of riches, fame, lust, pride, and self. Matthew 22:4 KJV says that though many are called, few are chosen. Not because God is picky, but because few truly repent. God wants all men to be saved and to come unto the knowledge of the truth.

Jesus said in John 20:21 KJV, "...as my father has sent me, even so send I you." As Jesus modeled, we too must do only what we hear our heavenly Father tell us to do through Jesus, through the Holy Spirit, and do it when God tells us to do it. By doing that, and by also speak only the words God tells us to speak, we walk in dominion fulfilling God's will. We also distinguish and discern the voice of our Father, and the voice of Jesus, the Good Shepherd, from the voice of a stranger (the Devil's voice) who will try to make his voice sound exactly like God's voice or an angel's voice (John 10:10—18, 25-29 KJV). In addition, we distinguish the voice of our own fleshy minds, once again keeping our bodies checked by our minds and our minds checked by our spirits as we walk in the Spirit of God by full faith in His love, not walking by sight or by our carnal senses. This is how we walk in Jesus' miracle-working dominion, His world-shaking authority, wielding God the Father's power and reflecting His glory with every demon spirit–binding, angelic spirit–loosing, sick-healing, captive-freeing, temptation-conquering, kingdom of God–reigning word of God we decree in faith!

Matthew 4:7 KJV says, "Jesus said unto him, It is written again Thou shalt not tempt the Lord Your God." This rebuke of Jesus underscores for believers the necessity to not only know the Word but to also continually renew our minds daily with the written word to distinguish the voice of God's sent word from the voice of the imposter, who also can quotes scriptures. Jesus was telling Satan, "Thou shalt not tempt or provoke or try to swindle Him who was in fact the Lord and God from the very beginning." Satan was quoting scriptures out of context as if Jesus was some chump who didn't know the Word. He *is* the Word!

Sometimes we as Christians can get impatient and try to hurry God's timing of deliverance from certain trials or breakthrough by repeating certain scriptures and praying more often and with a louder voice, as if God didn't hear them the first time. It is during this time that we would be much better served to labor to enter into the rest of God as revealed in Hebrews 4:1–3 and 9–11 KJV and trust that God knows, hears, and sees all our circumstances and knows our hearts concerning it. That doesn't mean we don't have to pray and ask God for our desires, but it means we are to pray in faith, pray earnestly as in Jesus' parable of the lawyers and then believe and have patience, trusting that God indeed wants you to prevail even more than you do. In Jeremiah 29:11 KJV, God reveals His heart for us. "For I know the thoughts that I think toward you, saith the Lord, thoughts of peace, and not of evil, to give you an expected end." God also said in Isaiah 55:9 KJV, "For *as* the heavens are higher than the earth, So are My ways higher than your ways, And My thoughts than your thoughts. For as the rain comes down, and the snow from heaven, And do not return there, But water the earth, And make it bring forth and bud, That it may give seed to the sower And bread to the eater, So shall My word be that goes forth from My mouth; It shall not return to Me void, But it shall accomplish what I please, And it shall prosper *in the thing* for which I sent it."

If you believe you have indeed received something, are you going to ask for it again? Then why keep praying to receive it just because you don't see it, feel it, hear it, smell it, or taste it? Remember, we walk by faith, not by sight. See yourself possessing it with the eyes of your faith, and just rest, saying, "Thank You, Lord, that I am in receipt of Your promise, and thank You for loving me and caring enough for me that as I hearken to Your voice and observe to do all that You say, all is well!"

The Third Temptation of Christ; Satan's Plea for a Deal

The third and final temptation of Christ in this post-Holy Ghost impartation of Jesus' wilderness saga is Satan's version of the Staples "Easy Button" marketing campaign. In Matthew's gospel account of Jesus' wilderness temptation, Satan's third temptation was the same one the apostle Dr. Luke revealed as the second temptation: the offering to Jesus of all the kingdoms of the Earth. Jesus had at this point during the wilderness temptations firmly clarified and established Himself as the Son of God, perceptive and keenly faithful in His sonship and perfectly content in His role as God's ultimate mouthpiece and power conduit on earth. Jesus was still coming for the Devil, as was prophesied, to destroy all the works Satan had put so much effort in erecting, his Babylon masterpiece, so the Devil figured on taking another shot at thwarting this whole redemption plan of God.

In the midst of this golden opportunity to seduce the Messiah away from His ever-so-clearly prophesied destiny, the Devil focused on plan C. Satan knows the Bible. He was there during the emergence and development of most of it, so most of Scripture is ingrained in his memory as firsthand experience and personal history. The Devil also knows that the Word of God reveals through prophecy that in the end, Jesus is supremely rewarded for His obedience through the entirety of His ordinance which included unimaginable suffering. His reward consists of, among other things, kingdoms and riches and glory from God the Father. Satan was astutely aware that Jesus knew of the torment, pain, and suffering beyond all natural human conceivability that awaited Him and in His flesh at least, Jesus dreaded the prospect (Isaiah 53:1-12, Matthew 4:8-9, 26:36-46, Luke 22:39-46 KJV). Satan realized that if these prophecies were to fully manifest, both Satan and his Babylonian world system were altogether doomed. This was likely the Devil's last best shot at tempting Jesus away from His destiny, so Satan pulled out all the stops. He offered Jesus the whole kit and caboodle of his worldly reign, the kingdoms of the earth, which incidentally weren't really his to begin with since he had swindled and stolen them from Adam. Nevertheless, they were indeed now in the power of the devil (Job 1:12 KJV), Satan's pitch now would be to convince Jesus that by choosing the Devil's plan, Jesus would also get kingdoms and power, but He wouldn't have to wait and wouldn't have to endure all that terrible suffering to get them.

That Devil is a super-sly trickster and a cunning and very observant predator. He perceived—correctly so—that if there was one area where Jesus would ultimately struggle, it would be in the knowing of the torment He would have to endure. So the Devil offered all the earthly kingdoms, which was a significant downgrade from the kingdoms promised by God, but the real temptation was in the fact that there would be no suffering for all the sins of mankind. Satan was apparently offering the Lord a kingdom reign but without all the betraying, suffering, flesh ripping, bone crushing, blood shedding, cross bearing, and wrath of God enduring, a very tempting offer indeed. No wonder Jesus was tempted. In fact, Satan knew from Scripture that the Lord would suffer some doubt but would ultimately overcome His trials (Isaiah 50:5 KJV).

The Devil's tempting offer would give Jesus another route to take to get the reward of reigning over His own kingdoms. The wording in Satan's offer was designed to sound similar to the promise the Father gave while avoiding the penalty for each and every sin of the world, sins that Jesus didn't even commit in the first place.

"How is this fair for You, Jesus?" I'm now paraphrasing Satan's temptation using imagination but alongside scripturally revealed truth to illustrate the devil's motive so we can learn the lesson of Satan's unchanging methods. He offers Jesus the 'easy button'. "Sure, Your sometime-in-the-future kingdom may sound promising, assuming the Ol' Ancient of Days remembers to give it to You. You know as well as I do that He has been around for … a really long time. As they say, the memory is the first thing to go. Oh yeah, and God even said in His Bible to put Him in remembrance of His word … See, Jesus? Dementia! It's happening already! I bet you don't even get to see that reward, that crown of life God promised. I bet He doesn't even remember where He put it. Have you seen it lately? One of those four beasts up there probably got a hold of Your precious crown by now and has chomped it to bits thinking it was a toy. So You see, Jesus? You would have to go through all that anguish and misery and gut-wrenching, soul-wrenching, merciless punishment You don't even deserve for a raggedy old chewed-up beast's toy of a crown. Or you could avoid all that pain, that categorical destruction, which you shouldn't have to face in the first place! All you have to do is bow down and worship me. In fact, shoot, J. C., you know what? I won't even make you--- You know, I was never really one for all those rituals and proper pious postures and such anyway. And as I recall, You are a bit of a rebel Yourself when it comes to religious rituals, eh? See, I knew I liked You for some reason ..."

Notice the familiar chumming up that is characteristic of the Devil's deceptive tactics. Satan wants to get inside your comfort zone, your circle of trust. "So check this out, homie. Since we are cool, and You know, bros and all, I won't even make You ... Uh, I mean, You won't even have to go down to Your knees or anything, J.C. Just bend forward and kiss this ring on my hand as a sign of Your loyalty to me and all these kingdoms are Yours Jesus. And oh yeah, You can even have this beautiful, delicious rack of barbecued ribs as a bonus so You can stop being hungry, starving, and all right now. You Haven't eaten in months and I can hear your stomach grumbling from a mile away. Let me help end Your suffering. Just kiss the ring, J. C. Just kiss the ring." Of course if Jesus had hypothetically taken his hand to kiss the ring, you know Satan would have lowered his hand down so Jesus would have had to bend over and ultimately kneel down anyway to kiss the ring, that old, slimy, filthy little...

It reminds me of that scene in the *Superman II* movie starring Christopher Reeves where one of General Zod's cronies had grabbed Lois Lane and threatened to kill her, tricking Superman into relinquishing his superpowers as a trade for Lois's life. Lex Luthor (Gene Hackman) was behind the strategy as Luthor informed General Zod that the crystal control center in the middle of the Fortress of Solitude would be able to strip Superman of his powers once activated. So Superman relented to save the life of his girlfriend, Lois Lane, and moped over to activate the crystal controls and then proceeded to enter the chamber. However, at the control center, Superman was able to change the process of the super power–stripping device so he was safe inside the chamber while General Zod and his cronies outside the chamber were stripped of their extraterrestrial powers. They could not tell they were duped however, because they felt no different. So when Superman stepped out of the chamber, he sheepishly sauntered over at the behest of General Zod, who raised his hand and motioned for Superman to kneel and take his hand as a sign of loyalty and devotion to Zod.

Superman took Zod's hand and tilted his head forward as if to bow as he began to kneel. The camera cut to capture the expression on General Zod's face as he relished every moment of his categorical victory, when suddenly, as Superman's knee was just centimeters from touching the ground, General Zod's satisfied, proud, cat-that-ate-the-canary, Cheshire grin instantly changed to a look of utter confusion mixed with searing pain as the bones in his now-ordinary hand were crushed by Superman's super grip. Superman finally revealed that he had double-crossed the double crosser in Lex Luthor and had rendered his nemesis, Zod, powerless and permanently without the use of his right hand, which he wouldn't be around for very long to use anyway. Superman promptly cast the lot of them into the great pit of the fortress. Sounds like recompense to me! The Holy Spirit did not see fit to dramatize the events of the wilderness temptation trials of Jesus. But if *Superman II* had been around back when the gospels were written, who knows?

Matthew 4:10 KJV, "Then Jesus saith 'Satan, get your sorry, lying, backstabbing, no good for nothing …'" That's probably what the Lord felt like saying. "Then Jesus saith unto him 'Get thee hence, Satan: for it is written, Thou shalt worship the Lord thy God and him only shalt thou serve.'" Notice that each temptation of Satan was met with Jesus' shield of faith together with the sword of the Word. Jesus displayed exactly how we are to express and enforce our victory over Satan. That victory is in Jesus himself as the Lord has already overcome sin. He showed His disciples and all believers how to navigate the dominion and power which the Lord gave to tread upon serpents and scorpions and over all the power of the Enemy (Luke 10:19 KJV). Jesus did not meekly hold His shield of faith limp-wristed, saying, "Father, Father, come help me, the bully Satan is after me again." Jesus stood firm and resolute in His royal Sonship, just as we believers are to stand firm and stout in our royal sonship with our helmet of salvation, the shield of faith, loins girt about with truth, the preparation of the gospel of peace and the sword of the Word always at the ready (1 Peter 2:9; Revelation 1:5–6, 5:10 KJV).

Jesus' faith quenched those tempting fiery darts soon after they came out of Satan's quiver. Those darts of doubt, mixed with lies and accusations may have indeed tempted the Lord, but they did not ensnare His mind, causing the Lord to dwell on His physical state. Jesus would not meditate on His circumstances or how bad He felt, or why all this was happening to Him, and why He had to be the chosen one. We know the drill of Satan's maneuvers. They are the same throughout the ages: sending thoughts of self-pity and sorrow, which can lead to sulking and pouting, often leading if unchecked to complaining and declaring the problems rather than the victorious truth. The Devil was not going to hear Jesus say, "Well, I'm Jesus, the Son of God, and no one else has to endure what I have to endure, so I deserve a day off. I wanna vacation … so why can't I just stay in bed till noon and get up and eat ice cream and watch old *X-files* reruns till I fall asleep?" Why couldn't Jesus just be selfish and not worry about anyone else? After all, even God can't cross His own edict of free will to make somebody choose Him.

God said, "I call heaven and Earth to record this day against you that I set before you life and death, blessing and cursing; Therefore choose life that thou and thy seed may live" (Deuteronomy 30:19 KJV). God not only displays our choices in front of us, but He also tells us what choice to make. He tells us which way to go because He loves us and does not want us to perish. He is our beloved Father, we are His beloved children so of course God wants to bless us beyond our wildest imaginations (Ephesians 3:20 KJV). Second Timothy 2:4 KJV says God would prefer that all men be saved and come to the knowledge of the truth. Yes we have a choice, but the choice is not as hard as the Devil makes it seem. The Devil is a liar.

People have a choice, and no one can make anyone choose one way or another, no matter how much they may love them, so why bother doing anything? What can one person do anyway, right? This is unfortunately the attitude of many people, even some Christians. The answer is love compels us to do our best to encourage the right decisions, reminding our beloved brethren of the eternal cost of making the wrong decision. A parent can't make her children choose correctly throughout their lives to be good citizens, but her love for them compels her to encourage and teach her children throughout their childhood to develop patterns of good choices. That mother knows the increased hardships that await a lifetime of habitually making bad choices, so love compels her to do her best to influence her children to choose right. That being stated, people may still choose the wrong way and choose to suffer the consequences or choose to not believe that their choices will result in added difficulties. When you have done all you can and given them information of which way is the right way to go, it is a situation that is no longer in your hands. They may even deny that your correct advice was accurate, even though it prophetically warned them. This stark reality is the true suffering with Christ's burden that we must bear, as faithful Christians. The endurance of suffering the knowledge of Christ is as Jesus revealed in Luke 22:28 KJV: "Ye are they which have continued with me in my temptations."

If the love of God is in you, then automatically you too love all men. Love every one—even the hard-to-love ones, you love them also. The desire for you to share and testify of God's love for the purpose of helping the lost find peace and doing all you can to encourage people to make the right choice by choosing Jesus is like breathing to you. If that is not the case, and your heart does not burn with desire to see those who are bound in their own mind and physically lame to get up and walk in the freedom of Truth, then it is likely Satan has successfully rendered you a placated Christian through doubt and cynicism. Satan relentlessly tries to beat us down, using our own faith, which he twists and perverts into fear, which makes his mirages and shadows manifest into our reality. Our faith is powerful, wherever we place it, which is why we are admonished by God to fear God and Him alone. Have faith in God, so as not to become one of the Christians who've said the sinner's prayer but who are now just skating by bouncing from one life tragedy to the next victimizing circumstance. Some are even trying to live as close as they can to the world, while indulging in the vices of the world and hoping to time it just right so maybe they can slide into the gates of heaven at the very last second. Unfortunately for those, there is a warning about how many will say to God at the great white throne of judgment, "Did I not baptize and cast out demons in your name?" The Lord will reply, Away from me, doer of iniquity, for I never knew you (Matthew 7:21-23 KJV).

Kingdom Nourishment for Spiritual Development

FINAL COURSE
CADENCE

So what's missing? Why aren't there more manifestations of the true sons and daughters of God for whom the creature and all of creation groans awaiting? The answer goes back to the effectiveness of the snare the Enemy has created in many of the minds of even born-again Christians. Satan has set up this world system, this Babylonian system so it would appear far too risky, too uncertain, too illogical (with the world's logic), too unpopular, and even too scary to make a firm decision to finally place our total faith in something we cannot touch, feel, smell, taste, see, and experience in a tangible way. All of our natural lives, practically from birth, have been based on and governed by laws that rule Babylon. We are taught from childhood that we are to hold on tightly to what we have for fear of losing it, to work hard, and then work even harder and longer for years, with the hope of one day getting a two-dollar pay raise and one extra vacation day. We are taught to save money when we can while at the same time we are compelled to buy the latest and greatest flat-screen television and the latest

$700 mobile phone on a two-year contract, the small print of which few ever even read. Before you realize it, people barely have enough to afford the increase in gas prices and maintenance on the vehicles, the mortgage or rent, bills, health insurance, health care, kids' braces, and everything else it takes to live in this modern capitalist society.

The mere thought of helping someone else in need and giving tithes back to God sends shame chills up most people's spines as they search their memories for that one time a year ago they happened to give fifty cents to someone on the street corner. Or the last time they donated some old, crusty clothes they didn't want anymore to the Salvation Army to make room in their closet for more stuff they bought but don't need and can't afford. Satan has successfully set up this Babylonian system to bog down most people, believers and unbelievers alike, in the busy-ness and tediousness of his worldly lifestyle constructs. The reason is simple: it is so when believers are presented with the truth formula for reigning as kings, queens, and priests having dominion over all the Earth, Jesus' admonition in John 14:12 KJV immediately gets relegated to the equivalent of a feel-good spiritual vitamin or a favorite gospel song people might play as they walk out the door to go do whatever their flesh wants to do.

Many Christians today unfortunately think they can just skate by doing the bare minimum of what it takes to be saved, trying to walk the tightrope of being a Christian but still loving and desiring things of the world. How dangerous a place that is to be where a Christian finds themselves enjoying living in the muck and the mire, of sin and carnality. "Love not the world," the bible says, "neither the things *that are* in the world. If any man love the world, the love of the Father is not in him" (1 John 2:15 KJV). When that state becomes someone's abode, they must instantly reach out and cry out from deep inside your spirit and call upon the name of Jesus. We must realize it is not okay to just waste away to dead men's bones on the inside while keeping up outward appearances. If a person professing faith in Jesus is returning and seeking comfort in their sin, repeating old carnal patterns, it is a clear warning sign. "But it is happened unto them according to the true proverb, The dog *is* turned to his own vomit again; and the sow that was washed to her wallowing in the mire. (2 Peter 2;22 KJV). They need the Lord to resurrect them and bring them back to life with the agape love of God. Keeping one's daily Christian walk moving forward using the weapons of our spiritual warfare become imperative. Inundating oneself with a myriad of busywork is just what the enemy wants and he will send as many things to occupy your mind as possible. Without spiritual perception through the close walk with the Father, the person becomes tempted to create a cocoon of excuses for the immobility of your Christian walk.

Even in these situations, Jesus is our perfect example to follow. After quenching Satan's fiery darts by walking daily by faith and not by sight (or the senses), and by continuing in constant communication with the Father through perpetual fasting and prayer, Jesus stayed well equipped to fight the good fight of faith (1 Timothy 6:12 KJV). The Lord proceeded to take the offense by speaking authoritatively and with understanding the precise word of God that addressed the specific attack and temptation, a perfect demonstration for how we disciples and believers are to respond to our trials and temptations. These temptations can be both physical and mental, but even the physical ones are designed by the Devil to create platforms for later mental attacks of condemnation. The Word of God, both written in the Bible and sent or proceeded (from the mouth of God) through the Holy Spirit or by God's holy messenger angels, is the perfect counterattack to Satan's temptations if they specifically address the area of attack. Jesus showed us how God's Word is to be used in conjunction with a very active and strong faith walk or march with cadence of purpose.

Cadence

While the shield of faith blocks the Devil's accusatory and condemnatory attacks on the mind, the sword of the spirit—the believer's offensive weapon, which is the Word of God—cuts to pieces the snare of the Enemy (Ephesians 6:17 KJV). The cadence is the diligent, purposeful consistency of the believer's faith walk, which resembles more of a march than a walk, particularly when a believer aligns themself with those whose cadence is intentionally headed in the same direction. When lined up in lockstep with the will of God, your Christian cadence keeps you confidently and effectively moving forward in the business of spreading and securing the gospel truth message of the kingdom of God, which must be priority one in the life of every Christian (Matthew 6:33 KJV)—not priority two or three or twelve, but priority numero uno!

Where a heavenly cadence persists, complacency cannot, for complacency quenches your spirit's fire, and that fire drives the engine of the kingdom-seeking Christian's cadence. No one is ever on fire to just maintain status quo. Without that cadence, before long the fire that motivates one to go out with the boldness and fearlessness of God's agape love for all mankind to lead the lost to Jesus and liberate those under bondage begins to dissipate. For the Christian who has allowed complacency to settle in and has let that fire dissipate, the heat has grown cold and the cold creates stagnation and rigidity. Stagnant Christians and rigidly stubborn, indifferent Christians are no threat to the Devil and his schemes. They are in fact a victory for him because in that state, these lukewarm Christians are certainly of no use to God. When the fire of God's love has been extinguished, it gives Him no faith through which to operate.

When fully engaged Christians whose march matches the cadence of their heart encounter a stale, stagnant Christian or spiritually stalled church that is frozen in the spiritual rigor mortis of religion, they can inject that Christian or church congregation with the elixir of God's agape love. The Lord will then reignite that spiritual fire within that church or brother or sister and cause them to rise and live again like Lazarus. God's love once again flowing through them will compel them to their calling and purpose, to action, and to the kingdom of God business of winning the lost and ushering them to Jesus, the door of the kingdom of God.

As we pray always with all prayer and supplication in the Spirit, and watching thereunto with all perseverance and supplication for all saints, we march daily in the purpose of God's will with the whole armor of God on, including having our loins girded about with truth and having on the breastplate of righteousness, having our feet shod with the preparation of the gospel of peace, and above all, carrying the shield of faith wherewith we may quench the fiery darts of the wicked, and taking the helmet of salvation, and the sword of the Spirit, which is the word of God (Ephesians 6:13–18 KJV). With this sword of the Word of God in the hands of the righteous, we wield the great power of God through His sent Word so in the face of all tests, trials, temptations, and tribulations, we cut to pieces the snare of the Enemy. For our weapons are not carnal, but they are mighty through God to the pulling down of strongholds and the casting down of imaginations and every high thing that would exalt itself above the knowledge of Christ. We bring every idle thought into captivity to the obedience of Christ (2 Corinthians 3:4–5 KJV).

As Christians live life with a cadence that matches the beat of God's heart, which is full of love and desire to see to lost saved and the bound free (1 Timothy 2: 4 KJV), we sync the cadence of our faith march to the frequency of heaven. The development of our synergy with the will of God the Father begins to leap forward as He transforms us, molding us more and more into the image of Jesus when we prioritize ordering our bodies to follow our minds and our minds to follow our spirits. When we order our spirits to then be subject to the Holy Spirit, subject to the will of God and the written and sent Word of God the Father, then and only then shall we faithful do the works Jesus did—and greater works. The time has come, and we will shall see greater works than these occurring now, in this time! Lift up your eyes unto the hills. Though God's promise, the vision is yet for an appointed time, but at the end it shall speak and not lie: though it tarry, wait for it; because it shall surely come, it will not tarry (Habakkuk 2:3 KJV).

Matthew 6:9 KJV says, "After this manner therefore pray ye; Our Father which art in heaven, Hallowed be thy name, Thy kingdom come. Thy will be done in Earth as it is in heaven. Give us this day our daily bread. And forgive us our debts as we forgive our debtors. And lead us not into temptation, but deliver us from evil: For thine is the kingdom, and the power and the glory forever, in Jesus name, Amen."

Select posts from the Cadence Of Heart
Ministries Facebook page.

Scripture references are from the King James Version unless otherwise indicated

What tempts your flesh is NOT your identity!

My heart breaks every time I hear someone identify themselves by their temptation. That is a lie strait from the pit of hell and a wicked trick by the devil! God gave us free will in hopes that we would chose to honor Him, not the devil or ourselves. Yes, He always knows which ones will choose Him, but He will certainly allow everyone to make that choice, themselves.

God did not create us to drink excessively so we WERE NOT born as an alcoholic. It is always our choice to make, whether to keep drinking, or end the seduction. Yes, we all have varying degrees of temptation to different worldy seductions, but GIVING IN TO THOSE SEDUCTIONS ARE ALWAYS A CARNAL CHOICE.

God did not design us to overeat. We were not created a glutton. We choose each time to keep eating all those horrible products that we know are bad for our health. We have a choice.

God did not create us to shiftlessly submit to every single lust that wafts across our nose. We were not born to just surrender to whatever seduction of the flesh comes our way.

That said, if you have made Jesus the Lord of your life, you are no longer a slave to the master of temptation. Having sex outside of the marriage covenant that God honors is a carnal-minded choice. Jesus is our strength in overcoming that temptation as long as our hope and faith remain in Him. That goes for both males and females. People are not born cheaters or promiscuous, it is a choice whether to give in to that seduction. People are not born to give in to the temptation to have sex with someone of the same gender. Regardless of the strength of our temptation, we all have a choice to make. The flesh is weak so if we try in the flesh to resist strong temptations, we'll fail nearly every time. The good news is as born again believers we are not by ourselves. We have a comforter who lives in us and who helps us. If we rely on Jesus and God's Holy Spirit, then our faith in the truth will make us free as we overcome all temptations by ABIDING in Jesus and walking after the Spirit, leading with our spirit instead of our flesh.

We were born to honor and Love God, not ourselves, not our flesh and our feelings. The moment we exalt God ABOVE our ego, our feelings and the desires of our flesh, we will find it so much easier to look to Jesus Christ as our help and thereby sail over your strongest temptations unburned!

Come out from under the charms of the kingdom of darkness and enter the kingdom of God! Salvation in Jesus the Messiah, the risen Savior of Nazareth is the door to God's Kingdom, and enlightenment by way of the Holy Spirit's revelation of Truth illuminates the way.

Relinquish all trace of the selfishness and pride which are at the very core of the kingdom of darkness. Pray and ask God to fill you with His Spirit to lead and guide you into all the Truth, AND HE WILL BE YOUR STRENGTH IN TIME OF NEED!!!!

You cannot shake hands while pointing your finger. Only seeking fault in someone will NEVER bridge the gap between you. If your pride leads more than your grace, then your motive is less than honorable.

Beloved,

Both racism and political party ultra-favoritism have zero place in the body of Christ.

The kingdom of God truth is that believers are all "Spiritual Jewish Christ-ocraticans". There are only the redeemed/born again/saved, and the unsaved. Period. We have work to do.

Do not lose focus, brothers and sisters. Race bickering is of the enemy, just like political party affiliation bickering. These are designed to take your eyes off of what really matters in these end times. Seek ye first the kingdom, both for yourself and the neighbor you are to love unconditionally and forgive repeatedly.

Please do not be seduced by it's intoxication. Father lead us not into temptation, but deliver us from evil! In Jesus' Yeshua's name!

When we the redeemed of the Lord speak the blessing of God's word/will in faith (nothing wavering) we open the portal and extend the royal carpet for the Holy Spirit to act.

In Genesis 1, the Spirit of God moved about the face of the formless void space. The instant God spoke His word in faith, "Let there be light." the Spirit of God began to create and formed the heavens and the Earth. God didn't have a question mark at the end of "Let there be light." There wasn't any need to shout either with an exclamation point. (Who would he shout to anyway?)

God spoke with the confidence of fact, period.

With what substance did the Spirit create everything out of a void?

With the substance of faith. (God's faith filled word.)

Hebrews 11; 1 Now faith is the substance of things hoped for, the evidence of things not seen.

Same principle applies to the believer who is filled with the Holy Spirit. You don't have Holy Spirit Jr. you have the one and only SPIRIT OF THE LIVING ALMIGHTY GOD LIVING INSIDE OF YOU abiding and waiting to hear us speak God's word in faith.

Learn God's word, it is His will. Speak it in faith, and you will become the sons of God for whom the whole earth groans awaiting.

Blessed powerful word of the kingdom!

Fear not!

Fear is Faith.

Fear is the BELIEF that something bad will happen.

Fear is having more faith that something bad will happen than faith that God is able AND WILLING to lead us not into temptation but deliver us from evil!

Jesus to Mary before the raising of Lazarus:

Did I not tell you fear not only believe and you will see the glory of God?

Jesus to the centurion, fear not only believe.

God to Joshua Be strong and of good courage. Fear not!

Job : "That which I FEARED has come upon me"!

Fear is faith, and is just as powerful, able to bring to pass that which we infuse with our faith. That is why we believers are not to fear the devil or the effects of his deceptions because that equals giving the devil your faith.

Our faith is the only thing that can give the devil power over us. Satan is indeed a spoiled and DEFEATED FOE, stripped of his power which he stole from Adam in the Garden of Eden. Jesus stripped the devil of the keys to death hell and the grave. THE ONLY POWER THE DEVIL HAS IN A BELIEVERS LIFE IS THAT WHICH THE BELIEVER GIVES HIM THROUGH FAITH. FEAR NOT!

Fear God!

Recognize God our Father as our faith personal trainer. He gives us faith weights in our lives to progressively build us up to where it doesn't matter what it physically looks like or feels like or sounds like, OUR FAITH IS IN THE SUPERIORITY OF GOD'S WORD OVER WHAT IT LOOKS LIKE OR FEELS LIKE! Then, get ready to see God use your faith to work the miracle of His truth in the physical situation.

Jesus to the woman with the issue of blood: WOMAN THY FAITH HAS MADE YOU WHOLE!

Matthew 4: 1-11

Matthew 21: 21

When God has used our life's wilderness trials to build up our faith, we redeemed shall go forth FULL OF THE SPIRIT casting out demons, healing the sick, raising the dead, preaching Jesus's already purchased deliverance to those held captives by the enemy's deceptions...doing the very works that Jesus did and greater works!

Fear is faith perverted. Faith is powerful wherever we place it. Keep your faith in VITA VERITAS VIA, Yeshua Hamashiach, Jesus the risen Christ of Nazareth!

Don't forget the most important meal of the day! The Word will feed your spirit! This bread of Life, this living water, will nourish you like no meat ever could, heal you like no pill ever could, and sustain you like no paycheck ever will!!!